THE STORY OF

CHELTENHAM

THE STORY OF

CHELTENHAM

ROBIN BROOKS

SUTTON PUBLISHING

First published in the United Kingdom in 2003 by
Sutton Publishing Limited · Phoenix Mill
Thrupp · Stroud · Gloucestershire · GL5 2BU

British Library Cataloguing in Publication Data
A catalogue record for this book is available from the British Library.

ISBN 0-7509-3213-9

Endpapers, front: Bustles in a bustling Promenade of the 1880s.
Back: Shopping in the Promenade in the 1970s.

Picture credits
The author would like to thank the following for permission to reproduce illustrations: John Whitaker p. 75, p. 106; Joe Stevens p. 87, p. 89 (top), p. 89 (bottom); Peter Stephens p. 88; *Gloucestershire Echo* p. 116, p. 117, p. 118, p. 119, p. 121, p. 131, p. 133, p. 135, p. 138, p. 139, p. 140, p. 141, p. 170, p. 182, p. 205; Brian Donnan Photography p. 213. Other pictures are from the author's collection. Thanks must also go to Bert Ashton, Josie Chilton, Brian Donnan, *Gloucestershire Echo*, Peter Stephens, Joe Stevens and John Whitaker.

'The Roar of Cheltenham' is reprinted by permission of PFD on behalf of The Estate of C. Day-Lewis. © 1973, C. Day-Lewis

Typeset in 10.5/14pt Galliard.
Typesetting and origination by
Sutton Publishing Limited.
Printed and bound in England by
J.H. Haynes & Co. Ltd, Sparkford.

Contents

ONE

Chinteneha

Around 1,200 years ago the Bishop of Worcester and the Bishop of Hereford were at loggerheads about which of them was entitled to the revenues of a monastery. The dispute was settled in AD 803 and the scribe whose job it was to document the proceedings wrote that the holy house was at Cheltenham in the kingdom of Mercia.

That's the first reference to Cheltenham, a Saxon name that means the village near a cliff. The word monastery probably gives the wrong impression. The building was likely to have been modest and home to a small group of clergymen who looked after a nearby church. Whatever it was like, according to tradition the building stood somewhere around Cambray until the end of the ninth century, when a band of marauding Danes, who'd sailed up the Bristol Channel and landed at Gloucester, arrived to destroy the place and steal whatever was worth taking.

The Domesday Book presents a brief sketch of eleventh-century Chinteneha and its immediate surroundings: there were five mills and prospering agriculture. At least 900 years ago there was a church occupying the site where St Mary's now stands – and only slightly more recently a manor house, which stood on land today occupied by St Matthew's in Clarence Street.

The names of four tenants of the manor, which appear in a survey of 1334, are recalled in present-day place names. Richard Munke is remembered in Monkscroft; William Fidler in Fiddlers Green; William Herte gave us Hesters Way; and land once farmed by Matilda Bayse came to be known as Bayshill.

Cheltenham was an agricultural community, never a centre of the wool industry like its Cotswold neighbours of Winchcombe, Northleach and Chipping Campden. The surrounding sandy soil was noted as 'very natural for carrots, cabbages and turnips', while nearby Leckhampton derives its name from the growing of leeks. Crops of oats and barley in medieval times were joined by vineyards and the area became a significant wine producer. Later tobacco was a major crop too. Before the land was enclosed into

The parish church of St Mary.

'Alpha House, Bays Hill' as shown in John Goding's 1863 *History of Cheltenham*.

'A long town having a market': the High Street.

fields, farmers cultivated it in long swathes – and evidence of the old strip system can be seen around the town to this day. Take a look at the lower slopes of Leckhampton Hill, for example, and you'll see the ridges and furrows quite clearly – especially in spring and autumn when the low sun teases long shadows from the ancient undulations.

In 1226 King Henry III granted Cheltenham the right to hold a market every Thursday, and 800 years on the town still hosts a market on that day each week. For centuries stalls were set out in the High Street. A reminder of those times can be found at an entrance to St Mary's churchyard in the town centre, where there's a pair of brass markers set into the pavement. These were originally used by traders to measure lengths of cloth.

But these events pale to insignificance when compared to the earthquake that hit town in the fourteenth century, when serious damage was done to St Mary's parish church and 600 local inhabitants were rendered homeless.

Curiously enough, natural phenomena seem to have been more spectacular in days gone by – at least according to contemporary reports. In the winter of 1643, for example, snow fell thick and hard for three weeks on the trot, accompanied by winds of such ferocity that houses were blown down. In June 1731 hailstones the size of tennis balls fell on Cheltenham, killing livestock and causing £2,000-worth of damage to property. Later that century, in 1793, a convoy of three wagons set off from Cheltenham bound for Tewkesbury and became trapped in a snowstorm of great violence. The drivers and horses all perished.

* * *

John Leland travelled around England and Wales in the mid-sixteenth century, recording what he saw along the way. At Cheltenham he found 'A long town having a market'. He also noted 'There is a brook on the south side of the town'. This brook was what we today call the River Chelt, but the river took its name from the town, rather than the other way round.

On some old maps the town's title is given as Cheltenham Street, for that's pretty well all there was of the place before the end of the eighteenth century. Until then Cheltenham comprised a single thoroughfare, following the course of the present High Street, with lanes leading off. Besides St Mary's church there were only a few stone buildings. The boys' grammar school, endowed by Richard Pate and built in 1578, stood in the Lower High Street between Bennington Street and Henrietta Street. Public business was conducted in the Booth Hall, standing on its stone pillars not far from the High Cross – roughly where the High Street now meets the Promenade. There was a prison, and opposite the junction with what is now Rodney Road stood an almshouse, described as 'stone with a chapel attached to it, a courtyard with grass in front – and a garden, pasture and orchard at the back'.

The Plough, sited where the Regent Arcade now meets the High Street, was one of a few inns, which with a court house, parsonage and sundry cottages comprised the town: 'One street continued with buildings on each side for a full mile.'

The medieval grammar school stood in the High Street, about where Tesco is today.

Old House, opposite Cambray.

To the north, between what is now Pittville and Swindon Road, was an area known as The Marsh. The headmaster of the boys' grammar school had the right to keep a cow on this common land, but more gruesomely, it was here that the town's gallows stood – and were sometimes used. The Marsh was crossed by Gallows Lane, which ran out to Prestbury.

In 1777 a Cheltenham footman named Joseph Armstrong poisoned his employer who'd discovered him stealing. Armstrong was found guilty of murder and hanged at the county jail. Then his body was returned to Cheltenham and hung in chains on a gibbet that had been erected on The Marsh – but not very well, because the gibbet collapsed and Armstrong's body fell to the ground. A local tradesman had to be hired to repair the structure. The body was left on public view for a year before the skull was bought by Dr Minster and the rest of the skeleton by Dr Newell, both Cheltenham physicians. The oak used to make the gibbet was acquired by the owner of Clonbrock House and recycled as gateposts.

Paintings of the town at this time appear to show a river running down the High Street, crossed by means of stepping stones, or a wooden bridge that stood at about the spot where the Famous gents' outfitters is today. In fact a river didn't follow this

The High Street with stepping stones.

course. But from the mid-sixteenth century the owner of Cambray Mill was required by local law to direct water from his mill pond to flood into the street for the purposes of cleaning. In a similar early attempt to improve public hygiene it was forbidden to wash clothes within 12ft of the water pump that was used by residents in the lower part of the town, as it was to dump animal skins and carcasses into the river.

Sir Robert Atkyns recorded in 1712 that Cheltenham boasted 321 houses and had about 1,500 inhabitants. This total was bolstered by Charlton Kings with 102 houses and 550 inhabitants, plus Leckhampton with 30 houses and 120 inhabitants. And that picture of a small, prospering, rural market town might well have remained essentially unchanged well into the twentieth century, had it not been for Capt Henry Skillicorne. One of the longest narrative plaques in the country can be seen in St Mary's church commemorating this Manx seaman, who began the development of Cheltenham into a fashionable spa.

*   *   *

Henry Skillicorne was the entrepreneur who turned the Bayshill spring into an attraction, but he didn't discover it. The land had previously been owned by Mr Higgs. He owned a meadow at Bayshill and on this land, at a spot close to where the Ladies' College stands today, a spring gurgled to the surface. Despite the fact that spas were very much the coming thing, Higgs failed to see the potential and in 1715 sold his land – spring and all – to a Quaker named William Mason. According to local legend, in 1716 pigeons pecking at salt deposits around the spring first alerted Mason to the water's special qualities, which incidentally is why the pigeon is a symbol of the town to this day.

Towards the top of quiet Crippetts Lane at Leckhampton stands a pair of ornamental iron gates. How they came to this remote spot is a mystery, but in about 1830 they stood at an entrance to Cheltenham's original, or Royal Spa. Perched on each gatepost is a pigeon. The bird also features on modern signposts found about the town.

Mason began to develop the spa by adding a bowling green and advertising the virtues of his spring's purging powers. In 1721 Mason leased the well to a man named Spencer at £61 a year and retired to Bristol. There his daughter met and married Henry Skillicorne.

All the while the fashion for spas was growing, despite contemporary cynics such as the writer Horace Walpole, who said 'People go to these places well and return cured'. Bath, Clifton and Tunbridge were well-established resorts. But Cheltenham received a boost when two doctors – Greville and Baird – gave a widely publicised, glowing report of its efficacious water.

*   *   *

In 1738 the shrewd sea captain set about exploiting the business opportunity that was bubbling to the surface on his land. First the spring was dug out to make a well, then pumping apparatus was installed. Over this was placed a canopied structure resting on four brick pillars. A small assembly room was built, with a billiard room over it. The area was landscaped, then, in the words of Skillicorne's diary, 'In the winter of 1739 I made the Upper Walk, planted elms and lime to the number of 37 and made a new orchard adjoining. The winter of 1740 I made the Lower Walk planting 96 elms at the

The town from Bayshill.

These ornamental gates in Crippets Lane, Leckhampton, once stood at the entrance to Cheltenham's original spa.

expense of £56. Had that summer 414 subscribers at the wells at 12 pence per piece. Built a yard round it and 18 little houses. The summer of 1740 was very dry. Had 674 subscribers at the wells'.

In that same dry year Dr Short's *History of Mineral Waters* was published, declaring Cheltenham's the best in the land, a recommendation that aroused national interest. Now things really began to take off. Short's praise prompted demand and the former sea captain's fortunes rode the crest of a wave as the reputation of his saline spa was carried to London and beyond in bottles. 'Visitors of great fortune and gentility' arrived to sip and a programme of entertainments was arranged for the well-to-do incomers. Balls and playing card assemblies took place, along with theatrical presentations staged at the theatre – converted from a former malt house – where a young actress named Sarah Siddons was discovered.

*   *   *

Opposite: Old Well Walk lined with elms and limes.

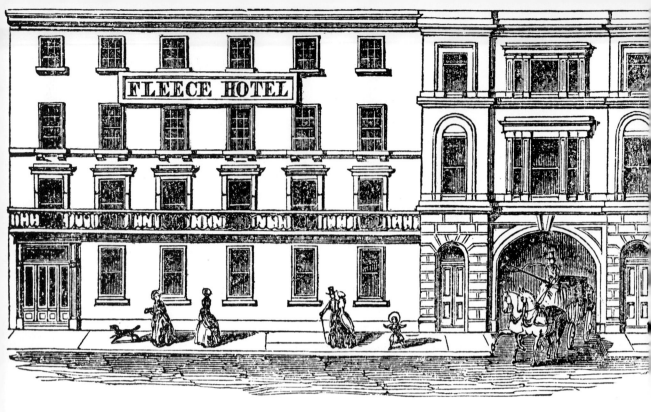

The Fleece stood in the High Street at its junction with Henrietta Street. A parcel delivery service by horse-drawn coach between Cheltenham and Gloucester operated from this hotel.

The number of visitors began to increase and more improvements to the well were made. Cheltenham was still no more than a one-street country market town, but it now attracted the rich and famous. Visiting celebrities included George Frederick Handel, Samuel Johnson, the poet William Shenstone and an array of aristocrats. On 11 August 1743, for example, the town was temporary home to a duke and duchess, one earl, five lords and ladies, two knights, a judge, two priors and a gaggle of gentry.

Residents of the town were bemused by the arrival of worthies from London and such distant parts and continued to stage entertainments of a rustic kind, such as cudgel matches ('He that breaks the most heads in these bouts and comes off clear, to receive a good hat and a guinea'), bull baiting and cock fighting – all of which took place in the High Street.

In the mid-eighteenth century the number of visitors declined. Twenty-four of the town's 300 houses stood empty and Cheltenham was in recession. There were three reasons why the town suddenly lost its appeal among the fashion conscious. Smallpox was rife, communications were poor and accommodation was sparse. As late as 1773 the town boasted but one lodging house and two inns. Visitors had to find rooms wherever they could, which often entailed moving out of town to Gloucester, Tewkesbury, Bishops Cleeve or Prestbury. The first recorded coach service from Cheltenham to London in 1738 completed the journey 'if God permitted in the short space of three days'. By 1770 a non-stop coach drawn by six horses ran the distance in twenty-six hours – an improvement, but still a daunting ordeal for passengers.

Transporting heavy goods to the town was a problem too. So following an Act of Parliament in 1792 work began to cut a canal from the Severn at Wainlodes to Coombe Hill. The idea was to provide a link with Gloucester Docks, so that stone, coal, timber and iron from the Forest of Dean could be brought by barge, then along the 5-mile turnpike road into Cheltenham. The canal opened in 1796 and for a few years made possible the spa town's building boom, but the venture was never the success it might have been. Having to transfer goods from barges at the canal terminus on to roadgoing wagons was inconvenient and slow, then in 1811 the Gloucester and Cheltenham Tramroad opened, rendering the canal redundant. The Coombe Hill canal remained in use until 1876, then fell into gradual decline.

Despite these drawbacks Cheltenham gradually geared up for the eighteenth-century tourist trade. A new theatre and assembly rooms were built, while older public buildings such as the Market House (which stood on stilts), butter cross and prison were demolished. Pavements and street lamps appeared.

The High Street was first lit by oil lamps in 1787. Gas lighting was installed in 1818 and replaced by electricity in 1891 when the town's first generating station opened in Arle Road.

In summer St Mary's parish church welcomed a well-to-do congregation. Services were presided over by the Revd Hugh Hughes, of whom a diarist wrote 'His stipend is £40 per year, which is considerably augmented by his skill at whist.'

In 1780 the controversial Simeon Moreau came to town from Bath. He aroused much resentment among Cheltenham's establishment by declaring himself Master of the Ceremonies and assuming control of social functions. An anonymous rhymster wrote 'Lately an ape in the shape of a beau/By the outlandish name of Simeon Moreau/Has officiously come at balls to preside/To preserve etiquette and pay homage to pride.'

Cheltenham's development as a spa continued in its sure but unspectacular way and might have continued to do so. Then in July 1788 George III arrived in town on the advice of his doctors, accompanied by Queen Charlotte, their three eldest daughters and royal hangers-on galore. The previous month the king had suffered what he described as 'a pretty smart bilious attack' and had been advised by his doctors that the health-giving qualities of Cheltenham waters would have the sickly sovereign fit and perky again in two shakes of an orb and sceptre. In fact the unfortunate monarch was suffering the early stages of a rare genetic disorder called porphyria. Besides biliousness, he displayed such first symptoms of this disease as irritating rashes, cramps and difficulty in breathing. Then came the onset of pronounced mood swings, so that George burst into tears for no apparent reason and soon after chattered away like a mad thing.

The illness developed quickly. On 19 November 1788 an equerry, who kept a diary of the king's progress along the road to insanity, recorded that George had talked non-stop for nineteen hours until his voice was hoarse. Perhaps worst of all, George knew his state of mind was in decline. 'I wish to God I might die,' he told his son Frederick, 'for I am going to be mad.' Shortly afterwards he attacked his son over dinner, before suffering convulsions and falling into a coma. A specially designed chair was made to restrain the king, which in lucid moments he referred to as his throne. In less lucid, more manic moments George was confined in a strait-jacket and subjected to cures prescribed by his physicians, such as having his skin blistered so as to let out the excess body heat. He died, deaf, blind and mad, in 1820.

But at least for the five weeks he was in Cheltenham, George seems to have enjoyed himself, quaffing at the well, strolling along the walks, going to the theatre and riding out into the countryside without a bodyguard (quite safely, as nobody recognised him).

The royal party also explored the surrounding area. Tewkesbury was a great favourite, and on their first visit the royals were introduced to Mythe Tute where they thoroughly enjoyed themselves. The king and queen were reported to have scrambled up the grassy knoll on their hands and knees like a pair of playful children. George liked

Opposite: Strolling in Old Well Walk was a fashionable pastime.

the Mythe so much that he returned twice more on 16 and 23 July and on one of these occasions made a surprise call on a local chap named Walker Wakeman. Apart from crawling about on his hands and knees, the king took a bracing walk from the Tute, over a wooden footbridge that spanned Paget's Lane and on to Mythe Manor. In recognition of the king's pleasure, the next Ordnance Survey map that was produced renamed Mythe Tute 'King's Hill' and the footpath 'King George's Walk'.

For five weeks the party remained in Cheltenham, living in a house at Bayshill loaned for the purpose by Lord Fauconberg. The royal visit thrust Cheltenham to the forefront of high fashion and celebrity. Afterwards its popularity as one of the land's leading spas was assured.

*　　*　　*

By the time their royal highnesses packed their bags to take the regal route back to London, Cheltenham was the most fashionable destination of the age. So much so that the list of notables arriving in town included '4 dukes, 3 duchesses, 6 marquises, 5

Bays Hill House was home to George III and the royal party when they visited in 1788.

Cheltenham was the most fashionable destination of the age.

marchionesses, 4 bishops, 10 earls, 8 countesses, 53 lords, 70 ladies – besides a host of honourables, barons, foreigners of title and other persons of distinction'. The latter group included, by the way, Jane Austen and Fanny Burney, followed by Paganini, Liszt, Charles Dickens and Oscar Wilde. Not all of them were impressed. Jane Austen spent three weeks here in May 1816 and returned later the same year with her sister to take the waters again. Apart from thinking her lodgings in the High Street outrageously expensive at 3 guineas a week, the visits seem to have left little impression on the novelist.

In 1821 William Cobbett, the celebrated author of *Rural Rides*, wrote: 'Cheltenham is a resort of the lame and lazy, the gourmandising and guzzling, the bilious and the nervous. A nasty, ill-looking place, half clown and half cockney.'

*   *   *

The Promenade connected the town with the Sherborne Spa, which stood where the Queen's Hotel now stands.

In the search to find more mineral springs and meet growing demand, new wells were opened. After the original Royal Old Well came the Montpellier Spa, Sherborne Well, Cambray Spa, Alstone Spa and Pittville. The oldest remaining example is found in Vittoria Walk. It was founded by a London banker named Henry Thompson in 1804. Thompson bought land on which the Montpellier and Lansdown estates were developed, and by 1809 had opened the Montpellier Spa – originally a wooden structure, later replaced by the grand, porticoed stone building that today is home to Lloyds TSB. The copper rotunda – 160ft in diameter and 60ft high – was a masterstroke added by the gloriously named London architect John Buonarotti Papworth.

A curiosity in the shadow of Papworth's verdigrised tureen is the drinking fountain topped by a fanciful statue of Edward VII, dressed in plus fours and a Norfolk jacket, apparently examining a young waif's fingernails. This was unveiled in October 1914 and was paid for by benefactors Mr and Mrs Drew of Hatherley Court, who devoted themselves to the rescue of old horses and seaside donkeys. Why was the statue positioned here? Because a century ago this was a rank for horse-drawn carriages. Thanks to the Drews, Dobbin and driver could have a drink while awaiting their next fare.

A nearby statue at the end of the main walk in Montpellier Gardens is the full figure of William IV. This first stood further down the Promenade in Imperial Gardens, but was moved to its present site in 1920. Pass this way on a Saturday morning and quite often

King Bill has been crowned with a traffic cone, presumably a little after closing time the previous night. While not wishing to condone such behaviour in any shape or form, it must be admitted that the impromptu headgear does cheer up the monarch's portly form.

*   *   *

On ground now occupied by the Queen's Hotel stood the Sherborne, or Imperial Spa, designed by the Jearrad brothers, local architects, who took as their model the Temple of Jupiter in Rome. The spa was connected to the town by the Imperial, or Sherborne Promenade. Why the two names were used isn't certain. But the significance of the venture is, because it established the route that became Cheltenham's Promenade – once eulogised by *The Times* as 'The most beautiful thoroughfare in Britain'.

But back to the Queen's Hotel, which was built in 1837 – opening a year later at a cost of £47,000. It occupied the site of the Imperial Spa, which was moved stone by stone lower down the Promenade to be reconstructed on the spot presently filled by Royscot House. Despite its magnificent appointments and opulent accommodation, the seventy-bedroom hotel was by no means an immediate success, and was sold in 1852 for a fifth of its original cost.

Over the years the Queen's has been a temporary home to a glittering array of notables and celebrities, including Prince Louis Jerome Napoleon, the Rajah of Sarawak and the Prince of Wales, later Edward VII.

It was on an official visit, however, in May 1897 that the Prince and Princess of Wales attended a banquet in their honour at Pittville Pump Room, where the courtly party embarked upon a luncheon of imperial proportions: Melon gonzalez, oeufs en cocette a la soubise, filets de sole l'Anglaise, noisette de mouton a l'epicurien, poulardes de Surrey, salade, jambon de York froid, delice de fraises glaces, friandises, peches, coffee, and five wines, an 1824 champagne and liqueurs.

What really tickled their royal majesties' tastebuds, however, were the biscuits made by George's – a local baker – as the *Daily Telegraph* reported on the day following: 'The Princess of Wales was much pleased with a dainty kind of biscuit, flavoured with vanilla, and honoured the maker with a request for the recipe.' This royal approbation did wonders for the baker's business and George's suddenly found itself the fashionable doyen of aristocratic nibblers. Typical was a note from the Duke of Manchester that read: 'Messrs. George Ltd. are requested to send as soon as possible two dozen tins of the biscuits approved by Her Royal Highness the Princess of Wales.'

*   *   *

Outside the Queen's Hotel is an ornate plinth that many visitors to the town must find bemusing. In summer months it is decorated with flowers galore, which – according to the words on the base – were 'Taken at Sebastopol'. In fact the grey, Victorian plinth is the survivor of a pair erected to display two cannons captured during the Crimean War. The Russian muzzle loaders were given to Cheltenham in recognition of its fund-raising activities during the conflict by Lord Panmure, the minister of war. For some time Panmure's gifts were stored in the stables at the Queen's Hotel. There was the inevitable squabbling about who should pay for the public monuments and it was not until the proprietor of the Queen's, Mr W. Davies, offered to put up some money that anything was done.

The cannons were eventually mounted on their splendid, much argued about plinths on 5 July 1858 and the wrought-iron arches of laurel leaves were added the following year. Then in April 1942 both big guns – with miles of iron railings that once surrounded the town's parks and gardens – were removed, supposedly to be recycled as armaments.

*   *   *

In the last quarter of the eighteenth century and first quarter of the nineteenth various spas, some small, some short-lived, opened and closed. One of the more unusual was Cambray Spa, an attractive, octagonal, gothic folly designed by the Gloucester architect Thomas Fulljames. It stood in what is now Rodney Road car park from 1834 and the original proprietor was Baynham Jones. Chalybeate – or iron rich – mineral springs had been discovered nearby in 1804 and, according to a contemporary guide, 'We cannot give a stronger proof of their efficacy than by noticing the rapid restoration of Sir Francis Burdett, Bart, who came to Cheltenham in May 1805 very seriously ill and deprived of the use of his limbs. The worthy baronet was restored in a few days and by persevering in drinking the waters and bathing the parts affected, left Cheltenham in the month of September in perfect health'. When the fashion for taking the waters dried up, Cambray Spa became a Turkish bath and remained so for the half century prior to its unfortunate demolition in 1938.

*   *   *

When the royal party left town in August 1788 Cheltenham's future was rosy. Five feverish weeks at the focus of fashionable attention had put Cheltenham well and truly on the map. Booming popularity promised expansion, greater celebrity and a new era of prosperity. Events abroad contributed to the boom. The French revolution of 1789 involved Britain in a war with the new republic which dragged on until 1815. This

Opposite: Cambray Spa opened in 1834 and stood in what is now Rodney Road car park.

meant that visitors who might otherwise have made for fashionable continental resorts came to Cheltenham instead. So did many army officers, serving and retired, lured by the town's reputation for genteel society and a gentle climate.

TWO
Spa-di-da
The Nineteenth Century

Cheltenham's spa society was at its most brilliant in the last quarter of the eighteenth century and the first of the nineteenth. Hundreds of new houses were built and expansion continued when the war with France ended. Favourable economic conditions heralded development on a scale hitherto unseen, and the town's resident population of 3,000 in 1801 grew to 20,000 by 1826. During this time Cheltenham was a building site and estates such as Lansdown, Montpellier and Pittville were thrown up in a frenzy of speculation. Most of the new buildings were of bricks dug from clay, moulded and fired on site.

Some of the finest early Victorian villas and terraces are found in Bayshill Road, Parabola Road and St George's Road. The Skillicorne family sold the land in 1837 to the Bayshill Estate Company whose directors were building speculators. Financial problems dogged the development, but over the next dozen years Royal Well Terrace, Bayshill Terrace and York Terrace appeared. So too did Royal Parade and – standing guard at the top of Bayshill Road – Queen's Parade.

Queen's Parade has the distinction of taking longer to be completed than any other building in Cheltenham. Started in 1839, work came to an abrupt end seven years later when the builder went bankrupt. The Corinthian-style pavilion at the west end wasn't finally added until the mid-1980s. It was at 3 Queen's Parade that Sir Arthur 'Bomber' Travers Harris GCB, OBE, AFC, LLD and Marshal of the RAF during the Second World War was born in 1892.

Just a stone's throw away is the Gordon Lamp. In 1885 residents in the area thought an ornamental lamp standard might brighten things up. Then later that year, when Gen Gordon was killed at Khartoum, the residents decided their lamp would be erected to his memory. A public appeal for funds was made . . . and £20 trickled in. As the chosen light cost £200 the organisers had to make up the difference. Then there was

Above: Like other grand estates in the town, Bayshill was developed by a group of building speculators.
Below: A £200 public appeal was launched to fund the Gordon Lamp, and £20 trickled in.

the question of who would bear the cost of illumination. The gas company quoted £22 per year, but the council said it couldn't pay more than £15, and suggested that only two of the three lamps should be lit. There were other problems too. The granite base was late arriving. The ironwork wasn't strong enough and had to be modified. And further expense was incurred when the lamp was converted to electricity in 1900. Because of all the wrangling, nobody remembered to add a plaque commemorating Gen Gordon until 1933.

*   *   *

Montpellier was developed by Henry Thompson and his son Pearson. It was laid out early in the nineteenth century with attractive villas and terraces surrounding spacious, ornamental gardens. In the 1830s and '40s specialist shops were built to serve locals and visitors and this quarter of town has retained precisely that character to the present day.

Montpellier Spa was developed by father and son Henry and Pearson Thompson.

J.B. Papworth designed Lansdown Crescent, but only nos 1 and 2 were completed to his plan. The rest were built with a cheaper, plainer façade by local architects Jearrads.

Most picturesque is Montpellier Walk, where properties are separated by caryatids. There are thirty-two of these armless and doleful looking ladies, based on classical Athenian statues. Two of their number date from 1840 and are made from terracotta, while the rest were copied locally later in the nineteenth century – all except one, made of concrete and added in 1970. They're not all the same, by the way. Some have their left leg in and some have their left leg out, as though doing the hokey-cokey.

Montpellier Arcade was built by the Jearrad brothers. The brothers also designed and built most of what we see today at Lansdown, when the original developer – Pearson Thompson – found himself in financial difficulties. Thompson had commissioned the London architect J.B. Papworth to design Lansdown Crescent – one of the few convex crescents in the country – but only nos 1 and 2 had been completed when the Jearrads took over the project. They dismissed Papworth, scrapped his design and completed the crescent in a simpler, less expensive fashion.

Royal Crescent was built between 1805 and 1825. The broach spire of St Matthew's church was removed in 1952, and the tower was lowered twenty years later.

Royal Crescent is Cheltenham's earliest string of Regency houses. It was built between 1805 and 1825 to a design of the Bath architect Charles Harcourt. In 1830, 18 Royal Crescent was home to the Duke of Gloucester, George III's nephew. He was visited by his cousin, the Duchess of Kent, and her daughter, Princess Victoria. It was the future queen's one and only visit to Cheltenham.

Lansdown Place was started in 1825 and the 'heart and honeysuckle' design ironwork on its balconies, cast in Falkirk, can be seen all over Cheltenham as well as in other towns. Work commenced on nearby Lypiatt Terrace twenty years later, in the Italianate style.

*   *   *

By far the grandest of Cheltenham's building speculations was Pittville, and in financial terms it was also the greatest flop. Its instigator was Joseph Pitt, a man of vision, ambition and terrible timing. He acquired 100 acres to the north of the town in the

The centrepiece of Joseph Pitt's vision for his new estate was Pittville Pump Room, a grand venture that bankrupted him.

early nineteenth century and judged that 1820, when demand for property in Cheltenham was at a peak, was the right moment to start constructing his dream. And what a dream.

Pittville was not simply to be an extension of Cheltenham. It was to be a new town. At its heart was a pump room to surpass all others, from which gracious villas would line the broad avenue sweeping down to the aesthetically satisfying conclusion of an artificial lake. Space was reserved for a grand crescent and a church, with tree-lined walks, rides and 600 houses in an assortment of architectural styles.

The architect of this planned grandeur was John Forbes, who set the tone of things to come by being arrested for forgery. Found guilty of trying to pass off a false bill of exchange to his local butcher, Forbes was sentenced to transportation for life. This was commuted to two years in Gloucester gaol, after which the talented Mr Forbes was never heard of again.

He *was* talented too, immensely so, because the Pump Room he designed is Cheltenham's finest Regency building. Here's a description of the town's architectural gem from John Goding's *History of Cheltenham*, published in 1863:

The spa has been pronounced the most beautiful and extensive establishment of its kind in Europe. Its first construction and the laying out of its drives – six miles in extent, cost half a million pounds sterling.

The building occupied five years in its erection and opened on the 20 July 1830 by a public breakfast attended by the leading families of the county.

The body of the building, which is 90 feet in length and 43 feet in breadth is surrounded by a colonnade 20 feet wide, the roof supported by fluted columns 22 feet in length and with capitals highly ornamented.

In the middle of the roof a figure of Hygeia is placed and the two wings ornamented with those of Esculapius and Hippocrates. In the centre of the building is an elegant dome, raised to the height of 70 feet.

Work started on the Pump Room in 1825; the building was intended as the visual and social focus of the Pittville development. Forbes is said to have taken as his inspiration for the building the Temple of Ilyssus in Athens.

A fanciful view of the town in the 1860s seen from Pittville.

Just off the ground-floor ballroom is the pump where spa water can be sipped to this day. A reading room, library and billiard room occupied the first floor (which more recently was given over to a museum of costume and fashion, until financial constraints forced the collection to be mothballed). Stand on the first-floor balcony, look down upon the grandeur of the perfectly proportioned, lavishly appointed room, and it's easy to imagine throngs of fashionable and wealthy socialites, the glitterati of the nineteenth century, milling around in the magnificent setting. The trouble was, they didn't. Or at least not enough of them to make the place pay. By the time Pittville Pump Room opened spas were passé. The rich and influential stayed away in their droves and Joseph Pitt's dream turned into a nightmare of unpayable debts.

The County of Gloucester Bank grabbed Pitt's elegant, but monumental white elephant of a building and sold it to Cheltenham Borough Council in 1889. Nobody knew what to do with the place. It provided the venue for the occasional flower show. A badminton club pinged shuttlecocks back and forth in the ballroom. And no maintenance was carried out on the fabric of the building.

During the Second World War the American Forces of Supply arrived on the scene. Nissen huts appeared in the grounds, Jeeps appeared in the car park and one of the

The Park estate was yet another speculation that ended in financial ruin for the developer.

finest Regency buildings in the provinces became a repository for tins of beans, rolls of lavatory paper, Hershey bars and such accoutrements felt by Uncle Sam to be essential for the invasion of mainland Europe.

When the GIs moved out after the war the Pump Room was in so decrepit a condition that it was touch and go whether the building would be razed to the ground or restored. Mercifully sense prevailed, and in 1960 the building was re-opened by the 7th Duke of Wellington, whose forebear, the 1st Duke, had been a familiar figure about town during Cheltenham's heyday as a fashionable spa.

Even though bankruptcy prevented the full realisation of Joseph Pitt's epic concept, Pittville is among the finest estates of its period to be found in the country. For proof, you need only glimpse Pittville Lawn, entered via its splendid gates, which date from 1830. Pittville Lawn was started in 1832 and building continued for ten years. It's a pleasing blend of formal terraces and individual villas, because would-be residents with the wherewithal were invited to build homes in a style of their choice. So they chose Greek revival, Gothic, Italianate, or whatever flight of architectural fancy they thought would impress the neighbours.

Wellington Square and Clarence Square are features of the Pittville estate that retain the elegance and tranquillity of a time gone by. Today you can wander in the peaceful gardens and admire the surrounding houses. In a previous age, however, each resident had a key to the private park their homes looked on to, and members of the general public were not permitted entry.

Ellerslie in Pittville's Albert Road was, in the early years of the twentieth century, home to the remarkable Rowena Cade. After the First World War this doughty lady left for Cornwall, where she bought a plot of cliff top near Lands End and spent the rest of her life building the Minnack Theatre – most of it with her own hands.

*   *   *

The Park area, a slightly later out of town development, was another grand plan that didn't quite work out as intended. Thomas Billings bought the 20-acre site in 1831 intending to open a zoo there, but the venture failed and he sold the land to Samuel Whitfield Daukes – the architect who designed Lansdown railway station and St Peter's church in Tewkesbury Road. The oval Park became pleasure gardens with a lake, walks and areas set aside for archery and cricket. Daukes built The Park's imposing villas and lived there himself in a gothic fantasy of a house he designed called Tudor Lodge, which was wickedly demolished in the 1960s. In 1931 the failed zoo and former pleasure grounds became St Mary's Teacher Training College, which in turn became a college of higher education and is now home to the University of Gloucestershire.

*   *   *

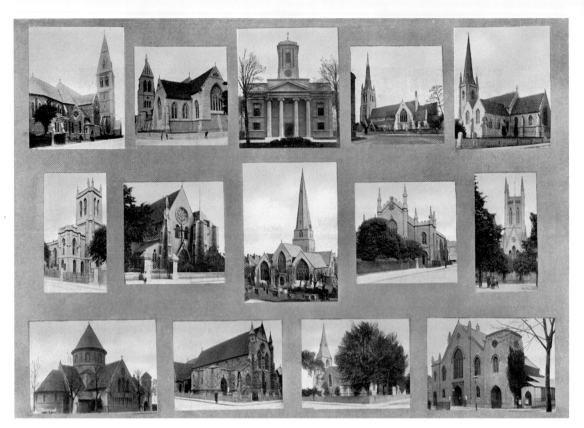

New churches appeared in the nineteenth century to meet the needs of the town's expanding population. Here are some of them, together with St Mary's, Cheltenham's oldest building. *Above, left to right*: St Matthew's, St Philip and St James's, St Paul's, St Gregory's Roman Catholic, St Mark's. *Middle*: Holy Trinity, All Saints', St Mary's, St James's, Christ Church. *Below*: St Peter's, St Stephen's, St Luke's, St John's.

In the mid-nineteenth century Cheltenham was growing apace. To cope with the burgeoning population, new churches such as St Mark's, St Peter's, Christ Church, St Philip's, St Luke's, St Gregory's and the synagogue were built.

At Charlton Kings the ancient parish church of St Mary's was packed to capacity and a new place of worship was plainly needed. There was strong feeling that the village's second church should be in Ryeworth or at Ham, locations that emphasised a separateness from Cheltenham. But no suitable site (that is, one that was affordable) could be found. The matter was solved in 1862 when Charles Cook Higgs – unofficial lord of the manor – gave land for a new church and £1,000 towards the cost of building it. He expressed the wish that the remaining finance should be secured by public subscription, but the good people of Charlton Kings failed to delve deep into their pockets. So then application was made for funds from the ecclesiastical commissioners, who didn't rush for the cheque book either.

In the end Charles Higgs paid the £7,000 building costs himself, a generous gesture indeed, but one he could afford. Higgs came from an old Charlton Kings family that traced its local roots back to 1500. The Higgs had acquired property and land around the area including Charlton House, Mill Furlong, Cudnall Street, the Ewens, Glenfall, Wellinghill Farm, East End Farm, Wagers Court in Balcarras Lane and fields along London Road. Charles Cook Higgs inherited the lot at the age of thirteen when his father died, and became quite a benefactor to Charlton Kings. Besides giving Holy Apostles' church to the community, he also established Higgs' Night School in East End Road, a building that today is used as the Scout hut. He built himself a fine house called Langton in London Road, which is now a restaurant.

John Middleton, a highly fashionable Cheltenham architect, was commissioned to design the new Holy Apostles' church. The house Middleton designed for himself in Overton Road is with us no more, but plenty of his Victorian Gothic work can be seen in town to this day – St Mark's church, Delancy hospital, the Ladies' College building in St George's Road and St Philip and St James's church being examples. Gloucester builder William Jones was engaged and the foundation stone of the new church laid in 1866. Work progressed slowly and plans for a tower and spire were dropped, probably on cost-saving grounds. Holy Apostles' was finally completed and opened by the Bishop of Gloucester in 1871, although it was not consecrated until 1885, by which time Charles Cook Higgs had been dead for a year.

For the first fourteen years of its existence Holy Apostles' was a daughter church to St Mary's in Charlton Kings and had no full-time minister of its own. This status changed in 1885 when Holy Apostles' became a parish in its own right, and vicar E.J. Bower was appointed as the first incumbent.

Work on the school building adjacent to the church began in 1871 and the architect was again John Middleton. Boys and girls aged between six and thirteen were educated separately, and in 1877 parents were required to pay 3*d* a week per child for the privilege. The school log tells us that for many households in this predominantly agricultural community the cost of keeping two or three children at school was prohibitive. School closed for August so that children could help with the harvest, and holidays were declared when travelling attractions such as Barnum & Bailey's circus, which visited in 1898, came to town. Diseases such as measles and mumps periodically kept a high percentage of pupils away from the classroom and more serious visitations – scarlet fever, whooping cough, diphtheria, 'brain fever' and smallpox – closed the school altogether from time to time.

*   *   *

Besides the grand, showpiece estates, more modest developments grew up. Mention South Town to most people in Cheltenham and they'll probably look blank as the name has fallen from use, but it once described the area that centres on Bath Road, bounded by Suffolk Square, The Park and the close weave of streets with their neat

A stroll with Nanny in Suffolk Square.

terraced houses that lie between. Building here began before 1820 and this was where the town's workers and tradespeople lived. Stonemasons and milliners, shopkeepers and furniture makers, coal merchants and bread bakers – many of whom enjoyed a drink, we may assume, for the area was well served with pubs.

Take a look at the building in Great Norwood Street, now converted into flats and previously a nearly new shop, and you'll notice that the downstairs windows are of etched glass with the words 'Smoke Room' in one and 'Bar' in the other. No prizes for working out that this was once a pub. It was called the Railway because a horse-drawn tramroad passed the front door on its way from Leckhampton Hill to Gloucester Docks. Limestone from Leckhampton quarries was brought to a yard directly opposite where it was dressed by masons before continuing its journey. Pastel-coloured houses and flats now occupy the ground where the stone workers once tapped away with hammer and chisel. Tram trucks on their way back from Gloucester docks carried coal to sidings off Norwood Road and there was a coal wharf in Bath Road at its junction with Clare Street. The site was a petrol station at one time, then a tool hire centre, and at the time of writing is about to be filled with shops and homes.

The houses either side of the former Railway pub are called Railway Buildings and were constructed in the 1890s by Stroud Brewery. To this day there is a clause in the deeds of these houses that alcoholic beverages are not allowed to be sold on the premises; after all, the brewery didn't want competition on its doorstep. There was plenty of competition nearby, though. Just inside Andover Street was the Andover Arms (now a private house) and just a short stagger round the corner to Painswick Road brought tipplers to the British Union, which in the late 1950s was renamed the Jolly Brewmaster.

Bath Road boasted no fewer than nine pubs within waving distance of each other. The Fountain stood where Somerfield's super-market is now. The Exmouth Arms, still in business, has a garden that was once called South Town's village green. The Brighton Arms was found on the corner of Suffolk Street and the Norwood Arms (now The Norwood)

The haunt of South Town's resident ghost.

looked down Bath Road from the Leckhampton end. The Brown Jug and Five Alls are still serving, but the Ten Bells between Exmouth Street and Hermitage Street isn't. What was until recently a delicatessen called Pam's Pantry used to be the King's Arms, and down on the corner of Kew Place was the King William Inn, opened by the Bavarian Brewing Company and inevitably known to locals as the King Billy until its closure during the Second World War.

Like other distinctive areas of Cheltenham, South Town has its resident ghost. The old man of St Philip's Street, so the story goes, is sometimes seen in the narrow alley that runs behind the terrace of houses, curiously carrying a gas mask. He asks lone passers-by if they've seen his dog; then, the question asked, a distant barking is heard and the spectral figure vanishes.

*   *   *

This building boom of estates grand and not so grand provided a great deal of employment, not only for construction workers but also for the allied trades, such as ironworkers, who were kept busy making railings, balconies and ornamental panels. For the best part of a century Cheltenham was known the world over for producing art metalwork, woodwork and statuary of the finest quality. The foundations for this reputation were laid by William Letheren, who established his Vulcan Iron Works on the site now occupied by Lansdown Industrial Estate in 1872. There he manufactured 'Improved lifts and cranes, iron roofs, girders, gates, railings, hurdles, casements, general ironwork, wrought or cast, mediaeval and artistic work in iron and brass'.

In 1865 Letheren won a competition organised by the Society of Arts Workmanship, then in the following year won again with an iron panel of such intricacy that the title of 'The greatest art ironworker in England' was bestowed upon him. His winning panel was acquired for the nation by the V&A. Such accolades prompted commissions from all over the world, and pieces produced by the local maker were shipped to Italy, South Africa, China and beyond.

Fortunately, good examples of the master craftman's work survive and can be seen locally to this day. Doric House in Church Road, St Marks, was home to William Letheren (who had two wives and twenty-two children, by the way) and the garden railings are the work of his firm. Other examples include the gates at Arle Court, St Gregory's, Leckhampton parish hall and the Town Hall's main staircase.

William Letheren died in retirement in 1910 – it's said of a broken heart – when the firm he founded went bankrupt. But the tradition of excellence in ironwork was continued by skilled craftsmen who'd worked at Letheren's, most notably Charles William Hancock.

Following the demise of Letheren's, the Vulcan Works were taken over by H.H. Martyn & Co. and renamed Sunningend Works. At first Martyn's concentrated on monumental masonry, but soon the company carved a name for itself in the allied areas of woodwork, panelling, sculpture, fibrous plasterwork, stained glass, marble carving, bronze casting and ironwork. Charles Hancock produced ironwork for Martyn's on a sub-contract basis. Then in 1908 the firm received a commission to make Marble Arch Royal Gates, and Hancock was brought in to open and manage a full-time art ironwork department at Sunningend. The gates, which took seventy craftsmen three months to make to a design by the Office of Works, included over 10,000 individually made laurel and palm leaves. Weighing over 40 tons, they cost £3,000 and were installed in 1908. Today they stand at the entrance to a national park in Saskatchewan, Canada, as they were removed from London in 1963. Examples of Martyn's ironwork can be seen all over the country and much of the world, but oddly enough there's precious little to be seen in Cheltenham.

Charles Hancock set up his own workshop once more, in Bennington Street, in the 1920s. It was here that he made the Bath Road entrance gates to Sandford Park and the ornamental canopy around Cobblers' Corner (opposite Littlewoods) in the High Street.

Ellenborough Hotel with wrought ironwork by master craftsman Charles Hancock.

One of his most spectacularly fine executions – the Ellenborough Hotel's porch – was lost when the building at the junction of Oriel Road and Wellington Street was demolished.

Richard Eede Marshall was another of Cheltenham's great ironworkers. He arrived from London in about 1822 and set up his manufacturing smithy in the High Street, adjacent to the passage near Boots that runs through to Albion Street. Later the firm moved to Royal Well Lane, where cars now park on what were half a dozen forge-workshops. Much of the firm's local work has been lost, including three massive stoves and two fireplaces at Pittville Pump Room, and the original gates to Churchill Gardens in the Lower High Street, which were scrapped by the town council in 1966. But there are still a few examples in town. Marshall's made the balcony railings at the municipal offices, the railings outside Beech House in St James's Square and the especially delicate ones at Oxford Parade in London Road. The firm was also responsible for the wrought chancel screen in St Philip and St James's church, which serves as a reminder that until only a few decades ago Cheltenham boasted a concentration of art craftsmanship without equal.

Ironworking was the nearest thing Cheltenham had to industrial manufacture. Without the factories found in other towns, the local economy rested on coach building, cabinet making, brewing and small-scale business. Domestic service was a major employer, along with opportunities in the growing retail sector.

*   *   *

Leckhampton quarries employed about fifty people and supplied stone for the many churches that were built in the town in the nineteenth century. Stone transported on a plateway was used to build Gloucester's Shire Hall in 1818, and via the city's docks reached building sites in fast expanding Bristol. Magdalen College chapel, Oxford, was also built of the local stone.

An enduring reminder of the days when Leckhampton limestone was quarried commercially is the Devil's Chimney. Numerous theories have been put forward over the years to explain the existence of this craggy outcrop. According to legend, the formation rises straight from the bowels of Hell. This view was supported by the local historian (and splendidly named) Thomas Frognall Dibdin, who in his *History of Cheltenham and its Environs* referred to the 'grotesque chimney, built by preternatural hands'. The notion that it was cut by Oliver Cromwell's cannon enjoyed currency for a time. And in 1897, in a book entitled *Cheltenham as a Holiday Resort*, the geologist S.S. Buckman – a respected authority in his day – explained that the Chimney was the result of 'natural differential erosion'; he calculated the feature to be between 400 and 500 years old.

You're welcome to believe any of these fancies, but the truth is probably more mundane. The Devil's Chimney is a remnant of the days when limestone was worked, from the eighteenth century up until the 1920s. The stone was durable and easy to carve; consequently it was popular for interior decoration work.

As quarrying gradually ate away at the escarpment, it became necessary to construct inclines down which stone could be hauled. In 1811 a tramway was built that ran from the top of Leckhampton Hill down to Daisybank. There were two lines – one for the truck loaded with stone to descend, the other for the empty truck to ascend. The trucks were tethered by a rope that wound round a pulley at the top, so that the heavy one going down pulled the lighter one up on the funicular principle.

From Daisybank the line dived to what is now Leckhampton Industrial Estate (the former tramway is now a public footpath, so you can follow its course if you're feeling energetic) to run along the west side of Leckhampton Road. That, incidentally, explains why the pavement is broad and in places recessed. At the Norwood Arms roundabout the tramway veered to follow Norwood Road, continued along Andover Road to

Opposite: The Devil's Chimney rises from the bowels of Hell, is the result of erosion, was cut by Cromwell's cannon, or is a folly from quarrying days, according to your fancy.

Westal Green, then on via Queens Road to Gloucester Road, where it joined the main Cheltenham to Gloucester tramroad.

It was the construction of an incline at the quarry that created the promontory on which the Devil's Chimney stands. The idea has been mooted that the Chimney was left because it happened to be a stack of rock that was too hard or too soft for commercial purposes. Its appearance, however, suggests something else. The chimney is simply too well proportioned to be an accident. Surely it was fashioned by quarry workers into its flue-like shape. The real mystery is not how the Devil's Chimney came to be, but why? We can assume that quarrymen didn't have a great deal of free time on their hands during the working day. And if there was the odd moment of inactivity, would they choose to amuse themselves by rudely chiselling a vast lump of limestone into the approximation of a chimney-stack? It doesn't seem likely.

In his book *Old Leckhampton* David Bick suggests that the Devil's Chimney was commissioned to attract publicity for Cheltenham as a growing spa and tourist town. The name Devil's Chimney first appeared in 1803 in a guide book titled *The Beauties of England and Wales*. If the curiosity on Leckhampton Hill was designed to be a motif for the town, the idea certainly worked. For two centuries or more the familiar outline of the chimney has been seen on publicity material for Cheltenham, and it remains one of the local sights to see for visitors to the area to this day.

Fears have been expressed that the landmark is about to fall down for over a century. The *Cheltenham Chronicle* reported that dangerous cracks had appeared when earth tremors were felt in August 1926. Then in the mid-1980s £20,000 was spent shoring up the teetering folly. On the subject of folly, by the way, thirteen members of the Gloucestershire Mountaineering Club climbed and stood shoulder to shoulder on top of the Devil's Chimney in 1959.

*   *   *

Cheltenham's origins as a centre for the financial services industry go back to 1850 when James Downing, who was the proprietor of a High Street drapery store, met with others at the Belle Vue Hotel in the High Street to found the Cheltenham and Gloucester Building Society. The Belle Vue Hotel is now called Irving House and was converted into flats some years ago.

A few more jobs were created when Cheltenham's first police force was established in about 1800. This was replaced forty years later by the county force, which had its headquarters in the town in St George's Place. In 1858 new headquarters were located in Crescent Place (now the Countryside Agency) and there the force was with us until 1970 when the present base in Lansdown Road opened.

*   *   *

The Cheltenham & Gloucester Building Society was founded in the Belle Vue Hotel.

The town only narrowly missed out on becoming a centre of the car industry. In 1893 Frederick Simms, a British business associate of the German engine maker Gottlieb Daimler, registered a company called the Daimler Motor Syndicate Ltd. His intention was to market cars in the UK powered by Daimler engines. Lack of funds forced Simms to sell his company to Harry Lawson in 1895. Then the following year Lawson launched the Daimler Motor Co., and set off with other members of the firm to find a location at which to begin production. They toured the country looking for suitable premises in a town or city where a pool of skilled labour existed, and after much searching a shortlist of two contenders was chosen – Cheltenham and Coventry.

In Cheltenham they located a factory that had belonged to the Trusty Oil Engine Co., part of a limited company called Weyman and Hitchcock. This firm had gone bust and the factory was available for immediate occupation, but Lawson and his fellow directors chose Coventry instead of Cheltenham. It's intriguing to speculate what might have been had the decision gone the other way. Daimler's presence in Coventry established a tradition for car manufacture that attracted numerous other marques to the area. Had Cheltenham been chosen by Lawson and co., the centre of British car manufacture could have been Gloucestershire, rather than the Midlands.

Horses provided some employment, one way and another. The Cheltenham Omnibus Co. was founded in 1890 and introduced the first horse-drawn bus route, which ran from Lansdown railway station to Pittville, a journey that was then priced at 1d. By the end of

In 1890 horse-drawn bus drivers worked a seventy-two hour week for £1.

that year six buses – some of them double deckers – were in service. Four were pulled by pairs of horses and two by but a single nag; the company had twenty-nine horses altogether. Eventually the route ran out of town as far as Swindon Village. Drivers, by the way, worked twelve hours a day, six days a week, and were paid £1 a week.

Cheltenham Riding School stood in Regent Street in the nineteenth century and there were at least two other riding schools in the town centre. In 1845 a dozen beginner's lessons at Reeves & Son's riding school in Montpellier were priced at £2 10s, while Smith's Livery Stables of Regent Street had the honour of providing the carriages for the Prince of Wales's visit in 1854.

* * *

For a snapshot of what it was like to be in Cheltenham during the twilight years of Queen Victoria's reign, let's take a stroll along Cheltenham's Clarence Parade using as our guide *The Cheltenham and District Post Office Directory 1891–92*. There's the *Gloucestershire Echo & Evening Telegram* office (still in the same place today) and close by is the auction house of C. Gostage & Co. A lodging house is run by Mrs Lacy and the chemist shop of J.A. Bennet is also where births and deaths are registered. Two tailors are in business, a brace of solicitors, one dressmaker and a malty whiff engages the nostrils as we pass Carpenter's Brewery. Professor of music Miss J. Macfarren gives lessons at her home, while J. Howett is a maker of chronometers, watches and clocks. Completing the hive of activity is the GPOA reading room. (What GPOA stands for we may never know.)

Half a dozen banks were found in Cheltenham – the Bristol & West of England, Capital and Counties, County of Gloucestershire, Lloyds, National Provincial and Savings Bank. If you had a letter to send, the General Post Office in the Prom (now Hoopers) was open from 7 a.m. to 10 p.m. Monday to Saturday and on Sundays from 7 a.m. to 10 a.m., then 5 p.m. to 6 p.m. There were four deliveries a day (only one on Sunday) and the stamp for a letter cost 1*d* (postcards 3 farthings). For 6*d* a twelve-

Lloyds Bank was built on the site of the Assembly Rooms in the High Street.

word telegram could be sent anywhere in the country. Carriers delivered packages to outlying parts and operated from town inns. So if, for example, you had a parcel for Gloucester, you took it to Mr Brown's office at the Fleece (which stood on the corner of the High Street and Henrietta Street) in time for the 11 a.m. or 6 p.m. run.

If infirm, or just plain lazy, you could hire yourself a wheelchair (known as Bath chairs elsewhere, but not in Cheltenham) from fourteen stands about town. Horse-drawn cabs were licensed to operate within a 4-mile radius of the Centre Stone (still to be seen on the corner of the High Street and Bennington Street) at 9*d* for the first fifteen minutes, then 3*d* for each additional fifteen minutes. Alternatively, horse-drawn buses operated between all principal hotels and Cheltenham's five railway stations (Lansdown, St James's, Malvern Road, Leckhampton and Charlton Kings). Anyone in a hurry might have preferred a one-horse fly, which carried two people at 1*s* a mile, or a pony carriage for 8*d* a mile.

*   *   *

There's been a theatre in Cheltenham for about 250 years. In 1758 an old malthouse in Coffee House Yard (off what is now Pittville Street) was converted into a place of entertainment; then in 1782 the town had its first purpose-built theatre, which stood in Grosvenor Terrace. A larger theatre was built in Cambray in 1805, but burned down in 1839. The Royal Wells Music Hall, later the Theatre Royal, opened in 1850 on the site

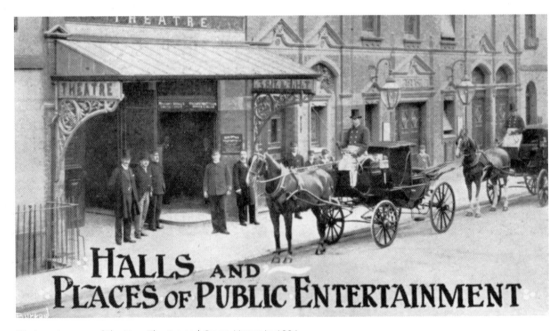

Lily Langtry opened the New Theatre and Opera House in 1891.

The New Theatre's sumptuous interior by Frank Matcham, who was also responsible for the London Palladium.

of Cheltenham's original spa. This was leased by the Ladies' College in 1887, then demolished and replaced with the Princess Hall.

The New Theatre and Opera House (now the Everyman) opened in Regent Street on 1 October 1891 with a performance by Lily Langtry. Small of stature, though huge of reputation, the celebrated actress took centre stage and delivered a specially commissioned (and very long) poem in rhyming couplets, which began:

> Hail Sylvan city, for thy vanished stage,
> With us at last – a golden age.
> Tis strange that Thespis hence so long should roam,
> Where could he find a more congenial home?

The theatre was designed by architect Frank Matcham – who was also responsible for the London Palladium – and built in just six months. Ellen Terry, George Robey, John Gielgud, Margot Fonteyn and numerous luminaries have performed on its stage, and the first talkie film seen in Cheltenham was screened at the theatre. This event took place in October 1929 and allowed local audiences to hear what Ronald Coleman's voice sounded like as he played the part of Bulldog Drummond. (Incidentally, the later Bulldog Drummond stories were written by Gerard Fairlie, who lived at Syde, near Birdlip.)

After the Second World War some bright spark had the idea of concealing the splendid, decorative brickwork of the theatre's façade under a coating of render. The theatre enjoyed mixed fortunes until it was bought by the borough council in 1955, then closed four years later. Fortunately an association of public-minded people re-opened the theatre in 1960, since when it's been called the Everyman. Thanks to a major rebuilding and refurbishment programme in the 1980s, the theatre looks pretty well as it did a century ago and is an amenity that deserves to be treasured.

Cheltenham's most famous thespian was Sir Ralph Richardson, whose father was art master at the Ladies' College. The actor-knight was born at 11 Tivoli Road on 19 December 1902. When he appeared on 'Desert Island Discs' he chose as his luxury a wind-up gramophone. 'Is that because you like music?' asked Roy Plomley. 'No, because I enjoy the exercise,' replied Sir Ralph.

On the wall in the pedestrianised area of the High Street is a blue plaque reminding us that Lillian McCarthy lived in a house near the spot. Miss McCarthy was a renowned nineteenth-century actress married to another celebrated figure of the Victorian stage, Harley Granville Barker. Lillian McCarthy was a favourite of George Bernard Shaw and took the female lead in a number of his early plays.

The town's main venue for balls and entertainments was the Assembly Rooms, which stood in the High Street on the site now occupied by Lloyd's Bank. It was here in July 1831 that Nicolo Paganini arrived to perform during race week, which that year took place for the first time at Prestbury, instead of Cleeve Hill. The formidable fiddler

Cambray House was home to Cheltenham Ladies' College from 1854 to 1873.

thrilled audiences at two sell-out concerts and, according to the *Cheltenham Chronicle*, his playing 'went off with great spirit, eclat and satisfaction to all parties' – so much so that Mr De Ville, manager of the Assembly Rooms, promptly booked Paganini for a third show. Unfortunately, the matter of money was not made clear.

As the auditorium filled with fans who'd paid twice the normal price to see and hear the great man, Nicolo argued that he should receive two-thirds of the door takings, while De Ville said 200 guineas was his best offer. Much miffed, the violinist stormed out of the hall and back to his rooms at the Plough Hotel. When the audience learned this they also stormed out of the hall and into the Plough. So threatening was the music-loving mob that Nicolo was forced to return with his Stradivarius and perform.

Entertainment and instruction were promised to an audience that packed the Assembly Rooms to hear Mrs Warrinor give a lecture on the benefits of wearing bloomers in 1851. However, when she appeared on stage dressed (not surprisingly you might think) in bloomers the audience was so outraged that most people walked out.

*   *   *

In the nineteenth century balloon ascents were a popular entertainment in spa resorts, and one of the first recorded in Cheltenham took place in 1825. In that year Mr Sadler

High Street in late Victorian times with the entrance to the Assembly Rooms in the left foreground.

came to town with his gas filled dirigible and an eager crowd gathered at Tramway Wharf (where Tesco now stands on the corner of Gloucester Road and the High Street) to watch the daring aeronaut rise into the blue beyond. Unfortunately he didn't, as insufficient gas was available to hoik Mr Sadler aloft. Rather than let his audience go home deflated, Mr Sadler was replaced in the basket by his sixteen-year-old son, and the lighter lad soon soared away to the crowd's delight. He landed in Chipping Norton some hours later.

Still more spectacular was the arrival in Montpellier Gardens on 3 July 1837 of the Great Nassau Balloon. People packed the park as the vast gas bag billowed, bloated and then floated over Cheltenham, wafting aloft Messrs Green, Moss, Spinney, Brunsdon, Hughes and Jearrad – all sensibly dressed in frock coats and top hats. The prevailing breeze carried them past Cirencester, to descend in Ashton Keynes at 7 p.m.

Balloon buffs had another treat later the same year, when on 22 September a launch was made from Montpellier Gardens. The balloon took four and a half hours to inflate, which must have tried the patience of the crowd, but few people went home as there was a novel twist to titillate the onlookers. In the main basket were a Mrs Graham and the landlord of a local pub (the White Lion) named Garrett, possibly making this the first mixed gender aerial ascent on record. And as if that were not enough excitement, a smaller basket was suspended from the main basket with a chimpanzee in it named Mademoiselle Jennie. Up the trio went, blown by a brisk breeze over the town. Then arriving above Lansdown the smaller basket was cut from the larger. Down below hearts stopped as the chimp-bearing basket plunged *terra firma*-wards. Mademoiselle Jennie was equipped with a parachute, but – and this added spice to the proceedings – the parachute had been designed by a Mr Cocking, who when demonstrating it only the week before had pulled his ripcord and met his unfortunate end when nothing happened. Fortunately on this occasion the 'chute opened and Jennie floated gently to earth. Mrs Graham and the publican came down in Hartpury, returned to Cheltenham and that evening a celebration took place in the Beehive pub, Montpellier Villas, where they were reunited with the chimp.

History was made on 3 October 1838 when John Hampton made the first successful parachute jump by an English person, from a balloon into Montpellier Gardens. Hampton announced that he intended to jump from a height of 10,000ft, but the town council stepped in and insisted, with a logic that's difficult to grasp, that he could only go ahead if he promised not to throw himself out of the balloon from a height of more than 1,000ft. Hampton agreed and took off. Then to the thrill of the throng he cut the tethering rope and allowed his balloon to achieve tremendous altitude before going over the side. His 'chute opened and contemporary reports tell us his feet touched the ground thirteen minutes later.

*   *   *

A far less exotic entertainment enjoyed by our Victorian forebears in Cheltenham is the age-old tradition of cheeserolling, which of course continues to this day. Each Spring Bank Holiday Monday this dramatic example of folk archaeology is played out on Coopers Hill. Crowds gather, as they have done for an unknown number of centuries, to take part in a local custom which is as curious as it is ancient. This strange business was probably going on in the days when Roman nobles lived in the villa at nearby Witcombe. And no doubt it was as incomprehensible to them as it is to the many visitors from abroad who flock to the spectacle today. The sight of people willingly flinging themselves down the cliff-like precipice in pursuit of a Double Gloucester cheese must do much to bolster the reputation England has for eccentricity.

By tradition, the yearly madness starts at 6 p.m. There are four chases down the one-in-one incline, a few races up it, and a tug of war. That's the main menu of events, but in days gone by more mysterious symbolism was attached to the occasion. When the maypole was erected at the top of the incline, for example, a bundle of gorse was tied halfway up the shaft. Why this was done is long forgotten, but it was part of the whole pagan ritual.

The remains of a 200-acre Iron Age hill fort's earthworks can be seen on top of Coopers Hill, so we know the spot has been inhabited for thousands of years. Unfortunately, of course, we don't know who the colourful character was who first had the idea of staging an athletics meeting on a one-in-one degree slope. But the origins of cheeserolling probably embrace fertility rites and a pre-Christian celebration of spring. This local custom is a relative of the egg rolling events that take place at the same time of year in various parts of Britain – and most famously in America in the grounds of the White House, since the custom was introduced in 1877 by the wife of President Maddison.

The first written reference to cheeserolling dates back to 1836 when the city crier of Gloucester announced the event. In the late nineteenth century cheeserolls were even more frenetic than they are today, with gypsy stalls, dancing, frolicking and high jinks. So many high jinks in fact that for a few years in the latter period of Queen Victoria's reign the cheeseroll was banned on grounds of excessive rowdiness, but it made a come-back, proving that it's impossible to stop folk being stupid if their minds are set on it. Not even the Second World War prevented the cheeseroll taking place, despite the absence of a cheese to roll. A pretend Double Gloucester was made out of wood.

Today an organising committee of local residents and volunteer helpers generally succeeds in keeping good order. A Master of Ceremony who wears the traditional white smock coat of a Cotswold shepherd, a top hat decorated with ribbons and carries a wooden staff always presides over the ceremony.

Since 1970 Coopers Hill has been the property of Gloucestershire County Council and each year the council receives calls from an assortment of individuals and bodies who want the event banned on various grounds (injuries, rowdiness, putting strain on emergency services). But the cheeseroll still goes on. It's not sponsored. Nobody makes any money out of it. There's hardly any prestige in winning. In fact, the entire daft business is devoid of reason, commercialism, or glamour. And many people think that's a good enough reason to keep doing it.

*   *   *

A gentler form of exercise, but one that widened horizons for many people in the nineteenth century, was cycling. According to faded newspaper reports of yesteryear, the first bicycle to appear in Cheltenham was ridden by Martin Rucker in the late 1860s. A pupil of Cheltenham College, Rucker won his first cycle race in 1869 astride a 36in boneshaker and went on to be elected captain of the London Bicycle Club. Another inveterate pedaller was the doughty Dorothea Beale, Principal of Cheltenham Ladies' College. In 1898, at the age of sixty-seven and despite hands stricken with gout, she learned to ride a bicycle and could be seen wobbling through the environs of Montpellier accompanied by a white-gloved page boy who was engaged to give her a push up the hills.

A two wheeler dealer duel took place in 1868 when Alfred Miles, a Cheltenham carriage and bicycle maker, threw down the gauntlet to his great local rival in the bike building business, whose name was Davies. A contest was arranged in which each rode a bicycle of his own making in a race between Cheltenham and Gloucester. On the day of the showdown Miles and Davies sat astride buttock-numbing bone shakers with wooden frames and iron tyres, the starting flag fell and off they scuttled. There was, of course, no Golden Valley by-pass in 1868; in fact there was no metalled road at all. So imagine what hardy types the two were to struggle along the 7-mile course in two hours, at the end of which they agreed to call the match a draw – and presumably had to stand up for a day or two afterwards.

Martin Rucker is said to have ridden the first bicycle seen in Cheltenham.

This event possibly began a long tradition of competitive cycling in Cheltenham. Back in October 1894 the town hosted a cycle race over a distance of 100 miles. The route ran from the Norwood Arms in Bath Road to Gloucester, Worcester, Evesham and finished on top of Marle Hill, then home to Cheltenham Football Club. The winner received a silver cup valued at 7 guineas.

*   *   *

The Cheltenham Croquet Club was founded in 1869, about the same time as Brighton's and the All England Club at Wimbledon, but croquet had been played informally in the town before that. It was

Dorothea Beale, Principal of Cheltenham Ladies' College and enthusiastic cyclist.

played by people with the time and money who held tournaments in their gardens. The notion of entering a tournament didn't exist then; it was a case of being invited to take part in a social assembly. Croquet gatherings of this kind were organised by Walter Jones Whitmore of Chastleton House, near Stow-on-the-Wold. He assured himself a place in the history of the game by formalising its rules and arranging Britain's first open tournament, which took place in Evesham in 1867.

Sports clubs met in Montpellier Gardens.

Before it acquired a home of its own the Cheltenham Croquet Club met at Montpellier. In 1898 the first tournament was held in Old Bath Road at the county cricket ground (now the East Gloucestershire Tennis Club). Then in 1904 the Croquet Club moved to its present site on land first rented from the Charlton Park estate, then bought for £800 in 1920. Early minute books reveal that club secretaries were faced with diplomatically taxing problems during the First World War. How, for example, do you advise someone serving in the trenches that his membership will be terminated unless his club fees are received post haste? Another delicate matter for the secretary was having to ask members to provide their own tea owing to war time shortages.

* * *

Cheltenham is nationally regarded as a bowls town. The many times world champion Tony Allcock is a local player and the town's clubs are thriving. It's a sporting tradition that goes back to 1883, when the Cheltenham Bowling Club was founded with its first green in Imperial Gardens.

In the early 1920s there was a move to start a new club for servicemen who had returned from the First World War. The borough council allocated a site in St George's

Cheltenham hosts the longest established cricket festival in the world.

Square, and the lush green with its half-timbered club house is an oasis of tranquillity in the busy High Street.

The Exmouth Bowling Club was founded by James Kitching, who took over as landlord of the Exmouth Arms Hotel, as it was then called, in 1890. A great enthusiast of the game, Kitching formed the club, played regularly in the team and became its treasurer. In its heyday the Bath Road flat green was reckoned to be among the best in the county, and the Exmouth Bowling Club succeeded in winning the Gloucestershire County Cup on one occasion.

*   *   *

Cheltenham Cricket Festival is a major event in the town's sporting calendar and has been since the first was staged back in 1872, when Surrey was the team entertained at the College Ground. The organiser of the cricket week, as it was then called, was James Lilleywhite of 3 Queen's Circus, and a three-day ticket for the game could be had for a princely two bob.

It was also the custom in those distant days to play a novelty game if the match proper finished early. In 1877, for example, a Gloucestershire *v.* Cheltenham match took place in which the county side used broomsticks and scored 299, to which the town replied, using bats, with a score of 50 for 2 when time ran out. On another occasion the great W.G. Grace of Gloucestershire and England took part in a novelty match held on a frozen lake in Windsor Great Park. Needless to say, even this unusual surface presented his prodigious talent with few problems. Grace scored a century and took 5 wickets.

Over the years county cricket has been played at other venues in the town. The East Gloucestershire Ground, Charlton Park, was used from 1888 to 1903, then the Victoria Ground hosted county matches from 1923 until 1937, and fans may remember that Gloucestershire played the Indian touring side at the Victoria Ground prior to the test series in 1986. But it's the College Ground that has always been home to the cricket festival, and the twin towers of the pavilion on the Thirlestaine Road side have provided the backdrop to many notable feats. In 1876 W.G. hit 318 not out *v.* Yorkshire. Twenty years later the county side were skittled out by Australia for 17 and Cheltenham-born Gilbert Jessop, said to be one of the hardest hitters the game has ever known, once slogged 51 in 18 minutes.

*   *   *

Perhaps the most remarkable sporting figure Cheltenham has produced is Fred Archer, whose life had all the dramatic elements of a TV mini series. The Cheltenham jockey rose meteorically from humble origins to widespread celebrity. This son of a publican was on first name terms with aristocrats and royalty. He earned vast sums and gambled big time. Scandal nipped his heels, with mystery and intrigue often taking a chomp or two too. Then came personal tragedy on a scale usually only encountered in works of fiction, and death by his own hand at the age of twenty-nine.

The first scene opens in 1857 with the birth of a son to Emma and William Archer of St George's Cottages, St George's Place, Cheltenham. Emma (née Hayward) was daughter of the landlord who kept the King's Head at Prestbury, while William was an ex-steeplechase jockey – a successful one at that. He won the Grand National in 1858 and rode in Russia for the Tsar.

Frederick James, as the new son was christened in Prestbury church, was one of five children. His father took over the King's Head and it was there that Fred at the age of eight saddled up for his first race, a challenge in a paddock behind the pub between the boy Archer on a pony and a local lad on a donkey. The donkey won, serving up a helping of defeat that Fred tasted infrequently on horseback. Apprenticed to Matthew Dawson, the leading trainer of the age, Fred's exceptional talent was recognised immediately. When thirteen years old he recorded 2 wins from 15 races. Two years later the tally was 27 wins from 180 rides. The following season came 107 wins from 422 mounts. And in 1874 at the pipsqueak age of seventeen he scored 147 wins to become champion jockey, an accolade he made his own for the next thirteen seasons in succession. Along the way he won 21 Classics, including the Derby on 5 occasions.

Even today, when sports personalities are hyped into icons at the drop of a six-figure sponsorship deal, it's difficult to appreciate what a star Fred Archer was. Princes and dukes jostled to hire the jockey, offering ever bigger fees to secure his services. Archer was seen with the great and the good, his every outing captured in newspaper column inches.

He raced in Britain, America, Ireland and France. The phrase 'Archer's up!' entered common currency, meaning 'success is certain'. And his marriage in Newmarket to Helen Dawson in 1883 was the most glittering, widely reported social event of the year.

Fred Archer branded merchandise sold in Spice Girls quantity. His gaunt features featured on mugs, mirrors, tea sets and chinaware, on medallions, toasting forks, pill boxes and brooches. There were portraits and embroideries and gift sets and kitsch-nacks galore (and some of them can be seen in Cheltenham Museum, by the way).

Described when out of the saddle as sensitive, gentle and modest, Archer became a demon on the track, merciless with the whip and foul mouthed, possessed by the will to win. This made him enemies who stirred up scandal, implicating the champion jockey in race-fixing coteries. The irritation of alleged shady associations may have worried at Archer's mind, but years of stringent dieting certainly took a toll on his body. At 5ft 8in he was tall for a jockey and fought constantly to keep his weight down. His daily diet was quoted as breakfast: a tablespoon of castor oil and half an orange; dinner: one sardine and half a glass of champagne; while in between these meagre mouthfuls the menu was purgatives, laxatives and steam baths. From the health angle this was a recipe for disaster, especially when liberally seasoned with personal tragedy. Fred's brother Robert – also a jockey – was killed in a race at Cheltenham in 1878. Then Fred's son died in infancy, followed within two years by the death of his wife while giving birth to their daughter Nellie.

On 8 November 1886 Frederick Archer shot himself through the mouth with his own revolver in the bedroom of his house in Newmarket. The coroner's verdict was that he had taken his own life while in a state of temporary insanity induced by typhoid fever. Perhaps the best memorial to this remarkable Cheltonian rests in the statistics of his career: 8,004 mounts; 2,148 wins.

*   *   *

In a speech about the country's haves and have nots, Disraeli coined the famous phrase about Britain being two nations. At the time he spoke the words Cheltenham was certainly two towns. In the great estates of Pittville, Bayshill, Montpellier and The Park, well-to-do residents exhibited the best traditions of Victorian, then Edwardian refinement. Former military men and civil servants retired to the elegant town, strolling along to the Promenade's New Club for brandy and soda reminiscences while their wives made up fours for bridge. But for others life offered only hardship. In the winter of 1878 the vicar of St Paul's appealed for help to relieve 4,000 poor in his charge. A general committee for the relief of the local unemployed was formed in the same year and distributed 18,000 quarts of soup to the needy in ten weeks.

Opposite: Fred Archer and his wife Helen. He was the greatest jockey of the age, but his life ended in tragedy.

The fashionable paraded themselves in Montpellier Gardens while the band played on.

A few years later Josephine Butler, the English social reformer and pioneer crusader for women's rights whose husband was vice-principal of Cheltenham College, wrote of the town: 'There are low class brothels and slums which would be a disgrace to London or New York; 12 or 13 of a family in one room, grown ups and children, girls of 15 carrying their own babies in their arms like bundles of rags.'

As early as 1849 Swindon Place (which ran between the Lower High Street and Swindon Road) was described by a Board of Health inspector as being 'without sewerage, carriageway or pavement: the gutter channels on the surface are always full of filthy fluid; and the place is never free from fever. Wanting in ventilation, the houses are always in an unhealthy condition'. Each house had a flagstone floored living room 14ft square in which was a hearth and oven. Upstairs were two small bedrooms. None had a bathroom, a few had mains water from a tap under the stairs, but most shared a communal pump. This slum along with others in the High Street/Tewkesbury Road area of town, or Lower Dockem as it was known, was cleared in the early 1930s at which time the rent on one of these less than desirable residences was 6s 6d a week. However, plenty of people in Cheltenham continued to dwell in mightily grim conditions until well after the Second World War.

*   *   *

The town's lack of industrial development meant that employment opportunities were always limited and resulted in significant pockets of social deprivation on the outskirts. If those who lived out of the town centre could find work at all, it was probably serving the needs of those who lived in the town centre. Charlton Kings, for example, was where Cheltenham's dirty clothes were washed and hung out to dry by the village's numerous washer-women.

On the other side of the coin, the very lack of factories and industry did much to preserve the town's aesthetic appeal as a leisure resort. George Rowe's *Illustrated Cheltenham Guide* of 1845 tells us the town boasted among its enterprises five newspapers, three brushmakers, five breweries, four banks, twelve chemists, fourteen grocers, four coal merchants, two stay makers, one cupper and a plumaissier (who made things out of feathers). In other words, Cheltenham was already developing as a centre for the service industries.

Beyond the boundaries of the town the surrounding area was still predominantly rural. This led to conflict between Cheltenham's traditional function as a market centre and its new role as a resort for the leisured classes. When the balance tipped from rural market town to posh and prosperous spa, the powers that be decided to tuck the peasants and pigs out of public view. So in the 1820s the market moved from the High Street to a new site. The entrance was a fantasy trio of exotic arches spanning what is now Bennington Street, which looked as though they'd been plucked from the palace of an Indian prince and dropped in Cheltenham by mistake. Over the middle arch were the words 'Centre Stone' and it was from this point that distances from Cheltenham to other towns and cities were measured. In 1867 the maharaja-style masonry was demolished and the Centre Stone moved to the nearest building, which was then a house, now Hinds the jeweller, where it remains to this day.

*　　*　　*

This fantasy trio of arches spanned the entrance to the market.

Some of the worst living conditions in Cheltenham were located at its west end. So it was appropriate, though coincidental, that it was here the town's first teacher training college was built, largely owing to the efforts of the Revd Francis Close who fervently believed that education provided the most direct route out of poverty. When it first opened, this place of education was titled the Normal College, so called because the schoolmasters and ma'ams it produced were expected to impart in their pupils the 'normal' – not high church – principles of Anglicanism.

Francis Close, who was curate of Holy Trinity church in 1824 and incumbent at St Mary's parish church two years later, was a tireless campaigner for all sorts of things. He railed against railways and if he'd had his way the age of steam would have taken a detour round Cheltenham. He was for strict observance of the Sabbath, against high church frippery and a heavyweight opinion former in the town. Close wasn't, of course, universally liked. Alfred Tennyson, who from 1843 lived for six years in a house that at the time overlooked St James's railway station, wrote of Cheltenham as a 'Polka, parson-worshipping place of which Francis Close is Pope'. Ruffler of feathers though he was, Close got things done. He opened the town's first Sunday school in Alstone in 1826, some half a century later than the country's first Sunday school, which was founded in Gloucester by Robert Raikes and the Revd Thomas Stock. Close also bullied and cajoled funds from public subscribers to open a number of day schools in town, one of the first being in St James's Square, adjacent to the former fire station.

To ensure that the high-church doctrines he disliked were kept out of schools, Close designed to put low church teachers into them. Presiding over a meeting to forward this aim, the ebullient evangelist declared 'that an institution for the training of masters and mistresses upon scriptural and evangelical principles in connection with the Church of England is urgently called for and that effort should be made to established such a training college in Cheltenham'. The plan bore fruit and in 1847 seven students, the nucleus of the new college, began their course in a rented house. Two years later the grand premises that can be seen to this day opened, occupying a 5-acre site in Swindon Road that had been donated by Miss Jane Cook. A chapel was completed and added to the complex of buildings in 1910. The foundation stone was laid on 1 April 1849 by Lord Ashley, Earl of Shaftesbury, and the architect was Samuel Whitfield Daukes, who was also responsible for Lansdown railway station, St Peter's church in Tewkesbury Road and the Royal Agricultural College in Cirencester.

Female students at the fledgling college first received training at the building in Lower High Street that had once been Cheltenham's hospital. In 1869 they moved to the newly built St Mary's Hall on the corner of St George's Place and Clarence Street. The architect who won the competition to design the female training department was J.T. Darby, who also designed Cheltenham Winter Garden. In the early 1920s the college's female department became St Mary's and by degrees established its campus in The Park. Then in 1961 St Mary's Hall was vacated and acquired by St Paul's men's

Bustles in a bustling Promenade of the 1880s.

college when it was renamed Shaftesbury Hall. The college sold the building in 1994 and the site was developed for housing.

*   *   *

The Cheltenham Directory of 1891–2 tells us that there were twenty-five elementary schools, including the Ragged and Industrial school in Milsom Street, a boys' orphanage in St Margaret's Road and a similar establishment for girls in Winchcombe Street, where 'The design of the institution is to board, lodge, clothe and educate destitute female orphans, particularly those descended from respectable parents'. Its intention was 'To instil into their minds principles of religion and morality. To train them up in habits of industry and cheerful obedience, to make them good household servants and to endeavour to teach them that the lowest stations in life may be rendered respectable by good principles and industry'. In other words it was a good thing for the masses to better themselves through education, so long as they knew their place.

Perhaps more enlightened by today's standards was the creche in Albion Street. 'The children of mothers who go out to work are here taken charge of and fed for 3*d* per day from 8am till 8pm.' The proprietor was Miss Gooding.

There were forty-six places of worship in Cheltenham and clergymen were more prevalent than any other profession, numbering 120 Anglicans, seventeen non-conformists, four Roman Catholic priests and one Jewish reader. Among the many

Above: Cavendish House opened its doors for business in 1823.
Below: The New Club sat elegantly at the junction of Oriel Road and The Prom.

trades listed were coopers, cork cutters, cycle manufacturers, organ and harmonium builders, livery stable keepers, plus rope, saddle and corset makers.

The Prom was mostly residential – although no. 13 was home to the Sanitary Inspection Association – and the town abounded in captains, majors, colonels, lieutenant-generals, generals and erstwhile military types. All of Cheltenham's residents – about 50,000 – are listed in the 1891–2 directory, from F. Abbott, a porter, of 16 Granville Street to Alfred Zebedee, a flyman (cab driver), of 6 Naunton Parade.

*   *   *

The High Street was Cheltenham in its original, rustic form. But the town's second incarnation as a fashionable resort is represented by the Promenade. Early in the nineteenth century, however, the land now occupied by the Prom was a marshy bog, boasting nothing more impressive than a few rather ramshackle cottages. In one of them, by the way, the widow of Spencer Perceval came to live after her husband had the dubious distinction of being the only British prime minister to be assassinated. (He was shot on 11 May 1812 by a Liverpool banker named John Bellingham, who was hanged for the crime eleven days later.)

The Prom – originally known as the Sherborne, or Imperial Promenade – began its existence as a walkway from Cheltenham's High Street to a spa pump room that stood where the Queen's now stands. It was laid out properly in 1818 and lined with forty-four chestnut trees. Then land along its length was sold for development and the first shop, a draper's called Clark and Debenham, opened for business in 1823. Messrs Clark and Debenham had another store near Cavendish Square in London and soon the Cheltenham outlet became known as Cavendish House. In the same year the store opened a grand building opposite, which originally had a wrought-iron porch and front garden with railings. It was home to a painter named Millet. When he packed his palette and brushes the house became the Imperial Hotel, then in 1856 the Imperial Club for 'resident noblemen and gentlemen', who also puffed havanas and passed the port at the New Club, which stood on the corner of Oriel Road – a site unhappily now occupied by the Quadrangle.

Perhaps the most photographed feature of the Promenade is Neptune's Fountain. This ornament is modelled on the Fontana di Trevi in Rome. It was unveiled on 3 October 1893, commemorates nothing and is in memory of nobody, but, according to a town guide of 1950, 'It was installed when Victorian Gothicism was on the wane, with beaux arts influences gaining ground on a lingering neo-mediaevalism'. So now you know.

Many buildings in Cheltenham are modelled on others elsewhere. The electricity sub-station, near the town library, recently converted into a restaurant, was inspired by the fifteenth-century Palazzo Strozzi in Florence. Joseph Hall, the borough engineer and architect of this unusual town landmark, which dates from 1894, also designed

Cheltenham's first electric street lamps – known as Onion and Dragon standards – and the Neptune Fountain.

The former Imperial Club became Cheltenham's main post office in 1874 and remained so until 1987. In that year the GPO moved to the High Street and Hooper's acquired the Promenade premises.

The town's first post office opened in 1800 at 127 High Street. The original post mistress was an elderly woman named Sally Saunders, who when once asked why it took five or six days to deliver post in the town, replied that she had better things to do than carry a letter to the bottom of the street.

The Municipal Offices, built in 1825, were originally private homes known as Harward's Buildings. Along the years buildings in the Prom stopped being homes and started being businesses. The end of the residential era came in the early 1980s, when an elderly Miss who'd lived at no. 121 for decades moved out, and Elgoods solicitors moved in.

The Town Hall was designed by the Gloucester architect Frederick Waller and built in the first years of the twentieth century to replace Cheltenham's previous main public venue, the Assembly Rooms. In an unsuccessful attempt to reverse the decline in popularity of Cheltenham as a health resort, the Central Spa was opened in the Town Hall in 1906. You can take the water there to this day, but you'll have to help yourself. No longer are there maids in mop caps and frilly pinnies to serve the salty solution.

At the same time, not far away in Bath Road, the Cheltenham Spa Medicinal Baths, in what is now the Playhouse theatre, offered a range of treatments, claimed to cure a medical encyclopedia's-worth of ailments.

To the rear of the Town Hall stood the Winter Garden – Cheltenham's own Crystal Palace. Built in 1878, this magnificent declaration of Victorian engineering prowess fell into disrepair and was demolished in the early years of the Second World War. One of the corner tower bases remains, however, behind the open-air bar in Imperial Gardens.

*   *   *

Cheltenham was two towns in the nineteenth century, one for the rich and one for the poor. According to contemporary accounts the latter group even came off worse when natural disasters struck. When the River Chelt burst its banks, inundating much of the

Opposite, above: Neptune's Fountain commemorates nothing, is in memory of nobody, but is the town's most extravagant item of street furniture.
Below: The town's main post office was found in the Prom when this photograph was taken in the early nineteenth century. The building today is Hooper's department store.

town in June 1830, the unfortunate Mr Russell, who farmed land that a century later was occupied by the Black & White coach station in St Margaret's Road, lost his entire crop of potatoes, all washed away. In 1840 another flood swept away the Hewlett Road house of a Mrs Aggs. Then just three years later a freak whirlwind zipped along Bath Road, plucking up a haystack en route, which was later found on top of Leckhampton Hill. A hurricane hit the town in 1851. Among other damage the gas works' chimney was blown over and the roof whipped off the portico of St James's railway station.

But for sheer strangeness, the curious natural disaster that befell Mr and Mrs Taylor on the evening of 13 July 1852 takes some beating. The Taylors were market gardeners by trade and were making ready for bed at their home in Rowanfield after a hard day's

In 1906 the Central Spa opened in the Town Hall where an attendant in starched white pinafore served the salty solution in glass tumblers. Today it's help yourself and plastic cups.

Montpellier Baths, now the Playhouse theatre.

market gardening when the first crashes of thunder broke overhead. Mr Taylor was already in bed, while his wife knelt at her prayers, when in through the open window shot a fire ball. The sizzling phenomenon passed between Mrs Taylor's legs, then struck the bed causing it to collapse (and presumably Mr Taylor to fall out). The fireball then collided with the wall of the house, which also collapsed, making the roof fall in. When the dust settled the cottage was virtually demolished. Mercifully, though, no injury was caused to the Taylors (except for singed thighs in the case of Mrs T), or to their children, who had been asleep in the adjacent room.

THREE

The Anglo-Indians' Paradise – 1900–19

Cheltenham crossed the threshold of the twentieth century with a population of a little under 50,000, which had grown rapidly in previous decades. Accounting for much of the increase were ex-colonial types – aging and impecunious – home from the Raj to eke out their dotage. Cheltenham was known as 'the Anglo-Indians' paradise' and had a reputation for being prim, poor and pretty. Scan through a town directory of the time and you find page after page of 'resident gentry' peppered liberally with colonels, captains, majors and generals. The town was in retirement and over the next twenty years the population fell.

The local economy was hardly vibrant. House prices had slumped and in 1901 there were 800 of the town's large houses empty or to let. Business could not have been brisk at the town's six banks – the Capital & Counties, Lloyds, London City & Midland, National Provincial, United Counties, and the Wilts & Dorset.

For those who could afford it, the Promenade's New Club (now Hooper's) offered 'permanent, supernumerary, temporary, extraordinary and honorary' memberships at 10 guineas to join, then 5 guineas per year. For those who could muster the energy there were clubs for such sports as polo, golf, badminton, croquet, cricket, rugby, football, swimming and water polo, bowling, archery, cycling, athletics, rifle shooting and angling. Recreation grounds were found at Marle Hill, Naunton Park, Whaddon and Barrett's Mill. Musical afternoons held in the Town Hall five days a week from 3.15 to 5.15 p.m. during the winter months were no doubt more to the taste of many. Churchgoing was a social necessity and the town's forty places of worship accommodated congregations of all persuasions. Leading the Anglican fraternity was the rector of Cheltenham – the splendidly named Revd F. L'Estrange Fawcett MA.

Education was provided by twenty-two elementary church schools, but another threshold was crossed in 1906 when the town's new education committee built Cheltenham's first state school in Gloucester Road.

*　　*　　*

Bicycles brought a new sense of freedom and broadened horizons.

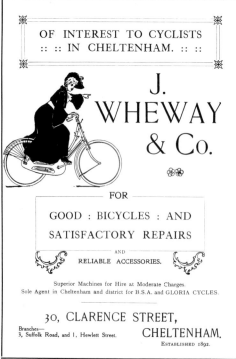

OF INTEREST TO CYCLISTS
:: :: IN CHELTENHAM. :: ::

J.
WHEWAY
& Co.

— FOR —

GOOD : BICYCLES : AND

SATISFACTORY REPAIRS

AND
RELIABLE ACCESSORIES.

Superior Machines for Hire at Moderate Charges.
Sole Agent in Cheltenham and district for B.S.A. and GLORIA CYCLES.

30, CLARENCE STREET,
Branches—
3, Suffolk Road, and 1, Hewlett Street.   CHELTENHAM.
ESTABLISHED 1892.

It was socially acceptable for women to take up cycling, as this advert of 1910 reflects.

Municipal concerts took place in the Town Hall every weekday afternoon during the winter season.

Fire fighting arrangements had long been inadequate, but in October 1906 the town's new fire station opened in St James's Square at a cost of £993. The brigade's horse-drawn engines included a steam-powered Merryfellow pump, which was donated by a public-spirited woman named Mrs Theobalds. A trio of tragedies kept local firefighters busy in 1914. St Paul's training college was gutted, fire inflicted £400-worth of damage on a timber yard in Knapp Road, and the west wing of Arle Court was set ablaze, as the *Gloucestershire Chronicle and Graphic* recorded. 'Despite the tempestuous weather, the inmates had to escape hurriedly in their night attire, three of the servants jumping from their bedroom window. One of them broke her arm and another injured her spine.' At the time of the fire Arle Court was owned by Herbert Unwin, a wealthy local businessman.

*   *   *

Visitors to the town had a choice of six hotels (the Cheltenham, Lansdown, Rising Sun, Queen's, Soyer's and Tate's), or rooms could be found at numerous lodging houses.

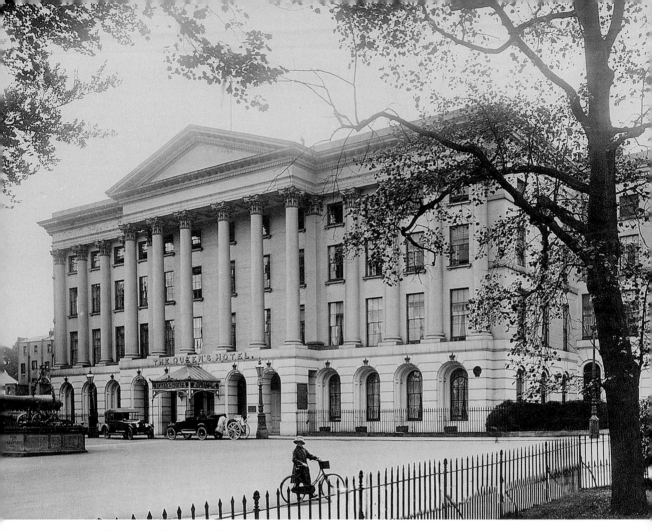

The Queen's Hotel fronted by Crimean cannons on plinths.

Few were attracted by the town's mineral waters anymore, but in an attempt to re-establish Cheltenham as a health resort the town council bought the Spa Medicinal Baths (now the Playhouse theatre) and promoted the facilities as a tourist attraction. This hydro-clinic peddled treatments for almost all known ailments, by the application externally (and, more ominously, internally) of the town's efficacious, saline waters. The sedative pool was for 'sleeplessness, chronic rheumatism and alcoholism', while an aerated whirlpool was 'for neurasthenia'. A paraffin wax treatment was claimed to do wonders for 'lumbago, myositis and fibrosis', while the contrast baths helped in cases of 'vaso-motor affections, foot swellings and chilblains'. Most exotic of all was the 'radio active mud bath – in great demand for the treatment of rheumatoid arthritis'.

The trade directory at the dawn of the new century also lists fifty physicians and surgeons, eight dentists, a dozen bootmakers, one gunsmith, four motor garages, two umbrella makers and seven restaurants. During the first decade of the twentieth century twenty-three pubs closed in the town.

Two orphanages – one for boys, the other for girls – sought to instil in parentless waifs the virtues of hard work, as did female refuges such as the 'Ladies' association for the care of friendless girls' in St George's Street.

*   *   *

In 1912 the Cheltenham corporation declared a competition, inviting local architects to submit designs for municipal offices up to a budget of £10,000. A site was set aside adjacent to the Winter Garden in Imperial Gardens and a prize of £100 was offered to the winning plan, with £50 for the runner up. It was intended that all submissions would be put on exhibition to gauge public opinion. But when the competition closing date arrived all eight of the entries received were costed at more than £10,000.

Harward
Buildings
became the
Municipal
Offices in 1915.

Consequently the corporation rejected the lot. At this the participating architects were miffed and complained that they had been treated shabbily, so the corporation grudgingly picked the best two, one by Healing and Overbury, the other by Chatters and Smithson, and gave each firm £20. The other half dozen entrants had to make do with a fiver each for their trouble.

All the designs were grand and imperial in scale, massive neo-classic monoliths, as was the fashion for civic buildings at the time when Britain ruled not only the waves, but those vast swathes of red on the world map that defined the empire. The design that most nearly met the corporation budget came from Pearson and Malvern in stone and ferro-concrete, at an estimated cost of £10,722. Perhaps keen for the business, this firm proffered a second design to be built on a site in St George's Square that was part-owned by the corporation. This too was rejected on grounds of cost, which was a mercy, as the land was instead given over to the bowling green that provides a pleasant open space in the centre of town to this day.

Deliberations continued until eventually the corporation bought the middle five of nineteen private houses in a Promenade terrace then called Harward Buildings. The £5,500 price tag, plus the estimated £3,300 for conversion into municipal offices, was paid for by a loan from the Local Government Board. The corporation moved to its new residence in 1915 and has remained there ever since.

*   *   *

For those whose names didn't appear in the 'resident gentry' pages, employment opportunities meant going into domestic service – and not much else. The retail sector provided some jobs, though: Cheltenham's leading department stores were Shirer & Haddon, with premises at Imperial Circus and the Colonnade, E.L. Ward's in the High Street, Cavendish House in the Prom and Drake & Co., which occupied premises on the corner of Winchcombe and Albion Streets.

Typical of its kind was T.B. Woodward's 'fishmonger, poulterer and dealer in game', an open-fronted shop at 1 and 2 Montpellier Avenue (which later in the century became Ron Summerfield's antiques shop). Hares, hams, ducks, pheasants, geese and more were hung outside to tempt custom in a way that would now make food hygienists reach for the smelling salts and a compulsory closure order.

One of the town's major employers with a workforce of about 200 was H.H. Martyn & Co., which in 1908 moved from its High Street premises to much larger works at Sunningend (now Lansdown Industrial Estate). The site had previously been occupied by Heyham & Hitchcock's Trusty Engine Works and William Letheren's Vulcan Iron Works.

SHIRER & HADDON, Cheltenham.

HIGH-CLASS

Dressmakers,

MILLINERS, :: :: ::
MANTLE MAKERS,
— and —

TAILORS AND
HABIT MAKERS,
MEN'S MERCERS.

General Drapers,

1, 2, 3, 6, 7, 8 & 9, IMPERIAL CIRCUS.
. . . PROMENADE, ⊕ CHELTENHAM.

House Furnishers,
and Decorators.

REMOVAL
CONTRACTORS.

UNDERTAKERS.

A LARGE COLLECTION OF SUPERIOR FURNITURE,
CARPETS, CURTAINS, ETC., ETC.

Furniture   Showrooms :—CLARENCE STREET.

H.H. Martyn gained a worldwide reputation for fitting out many of the finest and most famous ocean liners of the age, including the ill-fated *Titanic*. Four days out on her maiden voyage in April 1912, this flagship of the White Star Line struck an iceberg. Claimed to be unsinkable, the world's mightiest liner plunged to the bottom of the north Atlantic, taking with her 1,500 of the 2,340 passengers and crew on board.

The world was taken aback by the disaster, but the news must have been greeted with a particular sense of loss by Mr Moss and Mr Isher. These gents were neighbours in Rose and Crown Passage, off Cheltenham's High Street: together they carried out sub-contract work for H.H. Martyn. Mr Moss had built himself a lathe capable of turning tubes up to 15ft long and the mammoth machine was driven by a gas engine, which belonged to Mr Isher next door. Messrs Moss and Isher were commissioned to produce the ornately turned wood tubes that encased cast iron pillars in the *Titanic*'s public rooms. Imagine how their sense of pride must have given way to despondency when they heard the sinking news.

H.H. Martyn's woodworking department was also commissioned to produce timber frames under sub-contract to the London-based Aircraft Manufacturing Company, and fuselages were constructed for plane makers Maurice-Farman-Longhorn and Shorthorn, Bristol and Nieuport. Production took place at Martyn's Sunningend Works. However, demand for aircraft during the First World War soared, and soon Martyn's needed additional space. The firm took over the Cheltenham Winter Garden, and from 1916 until the end of hostilities fighter planes were made in the great glass-domed crystal palace of a building.

Cheltenham-born Alfred Martyn, son of H.H., realised that aviation was an industry of growing importance and wanted to be part of its future. So in June 1917 he founded the Gloucestershire Aircraft Co. (GAC) with capital of £10,000 in a joint venture between H.H. Martyn and the Aircraft Manufacturing Co. GAC went on to make some of the best-known aeroplanes in the history of aviation, including the Gladiator, Meteor and the Javelin. Growth was rapid and within six months the new enterprise employed 650 people making forty-five planes a week. A high percentage of the workers were women, whose skills were needed to handle, cut, stitch and fit the canvas with which aeroplanes were skinned. It was heavy-duty work. Stitching fabric on to a wing involved two women pushing a foot-long needle back and forth through the timber ribs, then tying and knotting the thread.

Women also worked in the dope shop. Dope was a spirit-based varnish used to stretch and seal the canvas. It gave off heady fumes and working in such an atmosphere must have been rather like sniffing glue all day. To ward off the effects each woman was given a pint of milk to drink at the start of each twelve hour shift, which was supposed to counteract dope-induced wooziness. For the privilege, women were paid £2 9s on days, £2 12s on nights. They also received a fortnightly examination by the company medical officer Dr Hebblethwaite.

The dope shop at Gloucestershire Aircraft Co.'s Sunningend Works, now Lansdown Industrial Park. (This photograph appears in *The Best*, the definitive book on H.H. Martyn & Co., by John Whitaker.)

By the end of the First World War the Cheltenham plane maker had received contracts worth £1.5 million from the Government. For its first two decades GAC manufactured its innovative aircraft in Cheltenham. In 1926 the firm name changed from 'Gloucestershire' to 'Gloster' Aircraft Co. as more and more business was being done with overseas customers who found the name and spelling troublesome.

*   *   *

Local news was dispensed in Cheltenham by five daily and weekly newspapers, which had a field day reporting an odd event that took place at 7.30 on the evening of 15 September 1904, when a gas explosion destroyed a shop in Winchcombe Street, reducing it to rubble. The demolished premises stood directly opposite Highbury Congregational church, on the site of which the Odeon now stands. From this address Mr Challice conducted his business, an unusual combination of taxidermy and carpet cleaning. When the dust cleared

Highbury Congregational church was where the Odeon now stands in Winchcombe Street.

the violence of the blast was revealed. Not only had the kapok been knocked well and truly out of Challice's shop, but the sturdy front door, blown from its hinges, was discovered across the road in the churchyard. Debris, including a selection of stuffed and part-stuffed animals, was scattered along the street. Fortunately no injuries were sustained, although a young woman was struck by an unidentified flying object. Police cordoned off the area, but trams continued to operate and were packed with sightseers. Oddly almost no damage was done to the neighbouring buildings, and even the Challice family home, Sudeley Cottage, which stood (and still stands) behind where the shop had been, was intact.

A less cheerful story concerned Sydney George Smith, who has the dubious distinction of being the only Cheltonian ever hanged in Gloucester jail. Smith lived in the town with Alice Woodman and they shared a miserable existence. He was rarely in work and the couple descended into abject poverty with their few possessions either sold or pawned. Unable to see a way out of their plight, Smith cut Alice's throat as she slept, then turned the razor on himself. Neighbours discovered him, severely wounded but alive, and called for help. The unfortunate man was restored to health, found guilty of murder and hanged on 9 March 1904.

*   *   *

A landmark disappeared in 1906 when Maud's Elm was felled. The venerable tree – 80ft tall and 21ft in diameter – stood in Swindon Lane and, according to local legend, marked the spot where Maud Bowen was buried having been wrongly accused of her uncle's murder and her own suicide.

The story has been part of local lore for centuries and concerns the tragic Maud Bowen who lived with her mother Margaret in a tied cottage in Swindon Village. Just turned twenty-one, she was handsome, kind of heart and industrious – as heroines in woeful legends often are. The Bowens were spinners and it was while taking the fruits of their labours to market in Cheltenham that Maud met misfortune. When she failed to return home by nightfall anxious Swindon villagers set out to search and at first light discovered the girl, face down in a stream, drowned. On a nearby bridge a second corpse was found, it was Maud's uncle Geoffrey with an arrow

Maud's Elm was said to have grown from a stake thrust through the heart of Maud Bowen after her suicide.

through his heart, fragments of his niece's dress clutched in his dead hand. The lord of the manor appointed a coroner to investigate, who soon returned the verdict that Maud had murdered Geoffrey and then committed suicide. As was the custom of the time in cases of *felo de se*, Maud's body was buried at the nearest crossroads with an elm stake driven through her remains. From this stake the tree grew that bore her name.

To add to Maud's mum's burden, she was evicted from her home by the lord of the manor. So it was that the distraught Mrs Bowen was sitting beside her daughter's grave when the heartless lord and his entourage passed on their way to Cleeve church for the baptism of his first-born son. An attendant was instructed to move Mrs Bowen on, but as he was about to manhandle her from the place an arrow from the bow of an unseen archer struck him down. An immediate search failed to find the bowman, so the villainous lord declared his attendant had been dispatched by an act of the supernatural and poor Margaret ended up in Gloucester jail charged with being a murderer and witch. Things got even worse. She was tried, found guilty and ordered to be burned on her daughter's grave.

The great elm was felled in 1906.

On the day of execution Margaret was tied to a stake and the kindling at her feet lit, as all the while the lord of the manor augmented the horror with shouts of derision and ridicule. Then at the height of the inferno's fury a crash rent the air and the pyre fell in on itself. When the smoke cleared Margaret Bowen had disappeared – and the lord who had added to her torment lay dead on the ground, an arrow through his heart.

Years later a lonely old man moved into the Bowens' cottage, venturing from it only occasionally to sit in contemplation at Maud's graveside. His name was Walter Baldwin and in his youth he'd been Maud's sweetheart. When the time inevitably arrived for the melancholic Walter to shuffle off this mortal coil, he revealed the truth of what had happened on the fateful night, long before, when Maud met her mysterious end.

The lord of the manor, it transpired, lusted after Maud and enrolled her uncle Geoffrey to help him abduct the girl on her way home from Cheltenham market. When attacked by the wicked duo, Maud let out a scream, which was heard by Walter who was hunting nearby. Rushing to protect his love Walter shot and killed Geoffrey, but the evil lord escaped, while Maud swooned, fell into the stream and expired. It was Walter who dispatched the attendant that rough-handled Margaret Bowen. And it was Walter who killed the real villain of the story – the lascivious lord – at Margaret's execution.

*   *   *

Opposite: Front cover of The pathetic story of the tragic legend of Maud's Elm, situate at Swindon, Cheltenham.

NEW AND ENLARGED EDITION.

THE PATHETIC STORY

OF THE

TRAGIC LEGEND

OF

MAUD'S ELM

SITUATE AT SWINDON, CHELTENHAM.

"The Murder of Maud Bowen!"

"Maud's Grave."

"The Wicked Lord de Vere!"

"Walter the Archer!" and

"Poor Old Meg!"

PRICE

2d.

BUILT-LEONARD, PRINTER & PUBLISHER, 6 & 7, BATH STREET, CHELTENHAM.

Contrary to its reputation for genteel inactivity, Cheltenham experienced riots in the early years of the twentieth century. The trouble began in 1894 when Leckhampton Hill, which had for centuries been a playground for the people of Cheltenham, was bought by Henry J. Dale, principal shareholder of the Leckhampton Quarry Co. Ltd. Dale outraged public opinion first by building Tramway Cottage on land off Daisy Bank Road that had long been the location for a fun fair each Good Friday. Next he fenced off 26 acres of the hill to which the public had always had free access, obstructed footpaths and even demanded that people whose property backed on to the hill should prove they had right of way to their homes. Dale's intention was to divide part of the land into exclusive building plots and retain the rest for exploitation by his quarry company, intentions that infuriated townspeople.

In March 1902 a group of protesters set off on foot from the central police station bearing banners such as 'Up hill to down Dale' and 'Hills can't be Dales'. By the time they arrived at Tramway Cottage their number was 10,000 strong. The mob tore down the hated fences and razed Tramway Cottage to the ground. Four ringleaders known as the 'Leckhampton Stalwarts', Walter Ballinger, Charlie Burford, Len Luce, and John Price, were brought to court and ordered to pay costs. As they couldn't, they were sent to Gloucester prison, to be released a short time later thanks to the *Echo*'s 'Shilling fund', which raised the necessary wherewithal.

For the next year or two the affair simmered. Dale erected more fences; Ballinger and his cronies

Cartoons in the local press demonised Henry Dale, owner of the Leckhampton Quarry Co.

Angry crowds tore down Tramway Cottage and other obstructions on Leckhampton Hill.

tore them down. But public sympathy was unanimous in the belief that Leckhampton Hill should belong to the people.

Things came to a head on Good Friday 1906. Led by the stalwarts, crowds once more gathered on the lower slopes of the hill to tear down Dale's obstructions and demolish Tramway Cottage again. Cheltenham magistrate G.B. Witts arrived and read the Riot Act. This time the Stalwarts were charged with 'riotously and tumultuously assembling to the disturbance of the public peace on Leckhampton Hill and there feloniously and unlawfully and with force beginning to demolish a certain house there situate'. Sentences of three and four months were meted out, though on their release the heroes were cheered at a celebration in their honour given in the skittle alley of the Wheatsheaf pub in Old Bath Road.

A court ruling, plus public pressure, eventually forced Dale to allow restricted access. This uneasy peace reigned until 1929 when the town council paid £6,500 to buy the hill for the people of Cheltenham.

*   *   *

The town's, indeed the country's, imagination was gripped by the ill-fated British Antarctic Expedition, led by Capt Robert Falcon Scott in 1911. The tale has a particular local poignancy, for one of Scott's closest companions on that cruel adventure was the Cheltonian Edward Adrian Wilson.

The son of a consultant at the General Hospital, Wilson was born in Montpellier Terrace on 23 July 1872. His family moved to a house at the Crippets, Leckhampton, and it was in the surrounding countryside that Wilson spent his formative years where he developed a keen interest in observing, painting and recording wildlife. He attended Glyngarth school, then the boys' college and went on to read science and medicine at Cambridge, graduating with first-class honours. Scientist, medical doctor, zoologist, accomplished artist, Wilson's academic talents were balanced by a cheery disposition and the ability to motivate the people around him, which was why in 1901 the invitation came from Scott to join his expedition to the Antarctic aboard the *Discovery*.

Wilson was 2nd medical officer on the four-year venture, during which he, Scott and Ernest Shackleton travelled nearer to the South Pole than any previous explorers and discovered a number of previously uncharted mountain ranges. On their epic journey the three men were forced to pull their own sledges when their dogs died. Then Shackleton fell ill and the party was forced to turn back.

Wilson joined Scott's second expedition to the Antarctic aboard the *Terra Nova* as chief of the scientific staff. A great deal of new scientific work was successfully completed before another attempt was made to reach the Earth's southerly axis.

Five men set out to conquer the Pole – Capt Scott, Dr Wilson, Capt Oates, Lt Bowers and Petty Officer Evans. The assault wasn't simply a matter of scientific endeavour or of personal ambition. Now, along with all their other burdens, the adventurers carried national pride, because a party of Norwegians led by Roald Amundsen, was also battling to be first to the Pole. The race was on. Despite their super-human struggle in appalling weather conditions, the British arrived at the Pole on 18 January 1912 to find the Norwegian flag already planted in the icy wasteland. Amundsen was the victor by thirty-three days.

Their energy expended by the useless dash for glory, probably less well equipped than they should have been and weakened by disappointment, Scott's explorers began the long trek back towards their base at Cape Evans. The weather was worse on their return. Food and fuel supplies ran low, illness and frostbite took their toll. Then to add to the misery Petty Officer Evans took a fall on the Beardmore Glacier and died soon after of concussion. Oates was the next fatality. Crippled and sick, but not wishing to spoil what chance there might be of his fellows reaching safety, Oates delivered the immortal words 'I am just going outside and may be some time' and was never seen again.

Scott, Wilson and Bowers were the last to survive, though they knew what their fate was to be, as the final entry in the leader's diary reveals. 'I do not think we can hope for better things now. We shall stick it out to the end, but we are getting weaker, of course,

The bronze of Edward Wilson who died in the Antarctic with Captain Scott.

and the end cannot be far. It seems a pity, but I do not think I can write more.' The three died huddled together in late March 1912. They were just 11 miles from a food depot. In November of that year their bodies and Scott's diaries were found in the small, snow-covered tent.

News of the tragedy did not reach Britain until February 1913. In Cheltenham a fund was immediately set up to build a monument to its famous son. The original plan was that two plaques, one for Scott, the other for Wilson, should be cast and hung in the Town Hall. Wilson's widow, however, intervened. She said that her husband, as a life-long nature lover, had always preferred to be outside. So instead of Town Hall plaques, a bronze statue modelled by Capt Scott's widow Kathleen was commissioned and placed on a plinth made by the local firm of R.L. Boulton & Sons in the Promenade's Long Garden. It was unveiled by Sir Clarence Markham, Arctic explorer and president of the Royal Geographical Society, on 9 July 1914.

*　　*　　*

Trams first trundled Cheltenham streets in 1901.

The town's tram era began on 22 August 1901, when two trams trundled from Lansdown Castle to Cleeve Hill carrying VIPs and local notables, the first passengers to travel on Cheltenham's new light railway. From the footplate of the first Union Jack bedecked car a bugler sounded the fanfare to announce the clattering convoy's advance. In its wake came a cheering crowd, on foot and bicycle, who watched as – reaching the summit after a steep one-in-nine climb – the glittering group of tram travellers disembarked for a champagne reception. The occasion prompted an enthusiastic response from the *Gloucestershire Graphic*: 'At last the trams are here! Round the corner comes a huge noise like a small Town Hall on wheels and the quiet respectability of Cheltenham is challenged by the sharp ting-tang on the gong and grinding of the wheels on the rail grooves together with the cars' singing on the wires.'

Britain's first tram was seen in Birkenhead in 1860. London's first ran in 1861, Gloucester's in 1879 and Bristol's in 1895. But Cheltenham was late to embrace the new mode of travel, as opposition groups voiced objections to the overhead wires, the noise and the dangers. Their predictions proved prescient. Two days before the system was scheduled to open, a tramcar descending Cleeve Hill on a trial run went out of control and overturned at Southam curve killing two workmen. It was discovered that wooden brake shoes for the American-made double decker had not been fitted. As a result of the accident the Board of Trade agreed to grant a licence on condition that only single deckers were used on the Cleeve Hill climb.

Once installed, however, the system found immediate favour with local people. In their first week of operation the town's trams carried 40,000 fare-paying passengers.

Boarding the burgundy with gold coachlined trams of the Cheltenham and District Light Railway Co. – the town's coat of arms proudly adorning each side – people discovered red upholstered seats in the downstairs saloon and wooden slatted reversible seats on the open-topped upper deck.

The initial stretch of track from Lansdown Castle to Cleeve Hill was just short of 6 miles long and took 120 workmen under four months to lay. For some reason Cheltenham's line had a 3ft 6in gauge, rather than the 4ft 8½in found virtually everywhere else.

In 1905 the system was extended to Leckhampton and Charlton Kings. A new loop line also meandered from St James's station, via Ambrose Street, into the High Street then up North Street, where a parcel delivery office was opened by the tram company in 1911. This was staffed by young boys who delivered packages to the door by hand, bicycle, or hand cart. They worked from 8 a.m. until 8 p.m. with an hour for lunch and one tea break of twenty minutes for wages of 5s a week.

Because of shortages during the First World War the town's trams received a coat of grim grey in 1917. Blackout restrictions also required that heavy drapes were fitted to the windows after dark and red paper caps were fitted over external lamps.

*   *   *

Town trams carried 40,000 fare-paying passengers in the first week of operation.

A mass of motor cars in Imperial Gardens for the 1,000-mile trial in 1900.

The days of tram travel were numbered from the time that Cheltenham's first motor bus, a single decker, entered service in 1912 on the LMS (Lansdown) station to Hales Road route. Then in 1924 four single decker Guys (each with the emblem of a red Indian over its radiator) began operating on the Lansdown–High Street–cemetery run.

By the end of the 1920s trams had been rendered redundant by the quicker, go-anywhere bus. Most tram services ceased in March 1930 and the town's terminal tram ran just after dawn on Wednesday 31 December of that year. The event was of such small public interest, by the way, that the *Echo* did not report the demise until five days later. The lines came up, the cables came down and most of the trams were scrapped. But a few could be seen around the town until about the mid-1960s. Two found their way to an encampment for travelling people in Badgeworth Lane. Another was used as a shed in a Staverton orchard. A market gardener at Swindon Village employed one as a store and another found its way on to Lilleybrook golf course. Perhaps some readers waited for a bus in the shelter, converted from a tram, that stood on Cleeve Hill at the point where tramlines had once terminated.

*   *   *

The first time Gloucestershire saw motor vehicles in large numbers was April 1900, when contestants in the Automobile Club of Great Britain and Ireland's 1,000-mile trial passed through the county. Cheltenham was chosen as a convenient stop-off stage midway between Bristol and Birmingham, and drivers of the eighty-three vehicles – which represented 10 per cent of all the cars in the country – had lunch at the Queen's Hotel. Forty-eight starters completed the course and the fastest time en route, a dashing 37.63mph, was recorded by Sir Charles Rolls. This half of the world's most famous motor marque was no stranger to these parts. In 1896 he drove from London to stay with his parents in Monmouth for Christmas. As he was steering his open-topped Peugeot up Birdlip Hill the engine stalled and the brakes failed. Rolls rolled back down the steep slope, gathering speed all the while, and no doubt looked distinctly pale by the time he reached Brockworth.

Cheltenham may have boasted more railway stations than any other town of its size. St James's was the grandest and stood on land opposite St Gregory's church, which was formerly Jessop's pleasure gardens. Besides St James's, the town's other stations included Lansdown, Malvern Road, Leckhampton and Charlton Kings. Until the early 1970s trains occasionally stopped during Gold Cup week at Hunting Butt station, Prestbury Park. And until the First World War there was a halt in the Lower High Street at the point where the bridge crosses close to the old gas works (now Tesco).

In the early years of the century the GWR submitted plans to build its main station in Townsend Street. The design was grand indeed, with a façade along the lines of Charing Cross in London, and to build it would have necessitated knocking down all

St James's station.

Charlton Kings station.

the houses on the east side of the street. Eventually the plan was dropped because of an argument with the town council over access. But the GWR was no stranger to building on a grand scale. When in 1908 the company constructed Malvern Road station with its curving main platform 700ft in length to serve the new Honeybourne line, hundreds of town people had to be rehoused. The development meant demolishing seventy dwellings in Great Western Road, Bloomsbury Place, Carlton Place, Hill View Cottages, Marsh Cottages and Whitehall Street. A pub named the Cherry Tree was knocked down too. The new line also cut through the old town cemetery and 300 bodies had to be removed to another resting place.

During the First World War Malvern Road station closed. It opened again in 1919 and in 1925 was renamed Cheltenham Spa. Another local station to be rechristened was Leckhampton, which opened with the completion of the Banbury line in 1881. Then in 1906 the Hatherley loop was added, enabling trains from the north to pass through Leckhampton on to South Wales. A train named the Coast to Coast Express ran before the Second World War. Starting on the LNER line from Newcastle, it joined the GWR track from Cheltenham and continued to Cardiff. It was at this time that humble Leckhampton station was given the grander title of Cheltenham South.

Charlton Kings station was designated a mere halt on Ordnance Survey maps – a touch derisory really, as the facilities included two platforms with a waiting room on each, a ticket office, gas lamps and a permanent staff. Until quarrying ended in the late

Above: Malvern Road station.
Below: Leckhampton (Cheltenham South) station.

1920s a line ran the 1¼ miles from Charlton Kings to Leckhampton Hill. An 0–4–0 tank engine named *Lightmoor*, built by the Bristol firm of Peckett's, chuffed along the branch line with locally hewn limestone bound for building sites in distant places. The sites of Charlton Kings station in Cirencester Road and Leckhampton station off Leckhampton Road are now both industrial estates.

*   *   *

The first locally recorded ascent and flight by a powered balloon took place in July 1910, when Birmingham-born E.T. Willows took off from Montpellier Gardens. His gas filled, cigar shaped craft was inflated inside high wind breaks and crowds gathered to watch. Anchoring lines were released and Willows, attired in gaiters, Norfolk jacket and a tweed cap, controlled the take off from his open, cage-like cockpit. A single propeller providing propulsion, the brave aviator was cheered in Cheltenham as he chugged off towards Gloucester. There he circled the cathedral tower before spluttering on to Cardiff in his small, motorised gas bag.

*   *   *

Crowds at the Athletic ground in Albion Street – and hardly a hatless head in sight.

The Gloucestershire cricket side of 1907 dismissed Northants for twelve runs. Centre front row is Gilbert Jessop, an all rounder of Bothamesque ability.

Eight thousand spectators packed the athletic ground in Albion Street to watch Cheltenham Rugby Football Club lose 18–0 to the New Zealand All Blacks on 6 December 1905.

The following year the town's cricket week, first staged at the College ground in 1872, became Cheltenham Cricket Festival. A giant of the Gloucestershire and England side was Cheltenham-born Gilbert 'Croucher' Jessop, who was born in Cambray Place in 1874. He was a pupil of the grammar school and succeeded W.G. Grace as captain of the county side. A formidably fast bowler and agile fielder, Jessop was reckoned to be the hardest hitter of his age. His twenty-year first-class career included eighteen test appearances and his 150 highest innings were made at the rate of 82 runs an hour.

Jessop played for Tewkesbury and Burford a few times. On the last occasion for the latter club he struck five balls so far outside the ground that none could be found. It was then that Burford had to ask Jessop not to play for them anymore as the cost of replacing the balls lost by his powerful strokes threatened to bankrupt the club.

A founder of Cheltenham's water polo and swimming club was Colin Lewis, who swam backstroke in the London Olympics of 1908 and was also a member of the gold medal-winning Great Britain water polo team.

* * *

Movie magic came to Cheltenham in 1908. A hushed silence fell over the gathered crowd in the Corn Exchange, which stood close to where Marks & Spencer is today, as the biograph, complete with two gas cylinders, was wheeled into the hall. Firemen with buckets of sand attended as stopcocks were turned, acetylene hissed and the machine's lamp burst into beam. The projectionist cranked a handle and *The Battle of Trafalgar* flickered on to the makeshift screen, accompanied by thrilled 'Aaahs' from the awe-struck audience. 'Rule Britannia' was played by the band as British, French and Spanish ships waged silent war. Nelson was hit. The audience gasped. He died. They wept. Then the band struck up 'Hearts of Oak' and, with a final turn of the crank, Britannia once more ruled the waves.

Cheltenham's first purpose-built cinema was the Royal Picture House in North Street, a 1,000-seater that opened its doors on 28 September 1914.

*   *   *

When an occasional day off coincided with reasonable weather, people in the town sought the simple pleasures of Liddington Lake, which stood adjacent to Leckhampton railway station. Open from 10 a.m. till dusk, from Easter Monday to the end of November, admission was 2*d* and the price included a trip around the island on a steam

Eversfield pleasure garden at Bishops Cleeve was a leading local leisure destination.

A cast of thousands and every one oddly dressed. The Gloucestershire Historical Pageant of 1908 was an Edwardian extravaganza.

launch. There were slides and rides and, when the lake froze over, as Liddington and Pittville Lakes both did in 1908, ice skating. Liddington Lake eventally closed in 1911.

Those able to venture further afield made for Eversfield pleasure garden, which was opened with entrepreneurial flair by the Denley family in 1900 at their home and 4-acre garden in Station Road, Bishops Cleeve. Leaflets advertising the new facility were sent out to Sunday schools, temperance groups and the organisers of works' outings with the tempting message that entrance to the swings, roundabouts and see-saws was free. Visitors paid only for their tea. Business received a boost in 1906 when the Great Western Railway opened a station in the village, just a stone's throw from the pleasure park.

*   *   *

Entertainment on a much grander scale was provided by the Gloucestershire Historical Pageant in July 1908, which took six days to perform, featured a costumed cast of hundreds and engaged ranks of massed musicians. This was a show of Edwardian grandeur at its imperial mightiest. A full-scale castle constructed in Pittville Park provided the backdrop, and against this performers presented no less than the entire history of Britain in word, mime and song. Composers Ernest Dicks, Lewis Hann and Heller Nicholls were commissioned to write music especially for the event. Dozens of horses were hired to carry medieval knights in full armour. Replica Viking longboats plied Pittville Lake. And Cheltenham went into a frenzy of pageant-mania.

The well-known catering firm of George's opened its Pageant Restaurant in North Street. Photographs of the individuals involved filled local newspapers. Souvenir spoons incorporating the borough arms enamelled in four colours went on sale for 2s 6d, or 5 bob for the solid silver version. A pageant lunch at the Town Hall was attended by the Lord Mayor of London. And in the same venue a pageant fancy dress competition was arranged, which was won by Mr R.H. Thakeray who went as a Zulu chief.

Organising the pageant was a committee of over 100 people under the chairmanship of His Worship The Mayor of Cheltenham George Dimmer, with umpteen more subcommittees responsible for music, design, dance, costume, accommodation and much else. Master of the pageant was Mr G.P. Hawtrey, who at the opening ceremony welcomed Lord Roberts VC, supported by a mounted guard of honour provided by the 5th Battalion Gloucestershire Regiment, to declare the proceedings under way. Lord

These performers appeared in Episode III of the 1908 pageant, in which the struggle of ecclesiasticism against kingly power in Saxon times was depicted.

The pageant's grand finale involved the entire cast, marching and singing, augmented by a choir in boats on Pittville lake dressed as everything from Vikings to Eton schoolboys.

Roberts looked like a pageant on his own. The esteemed veteran of the Indian Mutiny, Afghanistan and the Boer Wars wore a mile or two of gold braid, a museum's worth of medals and a helmet apparently topped by the plumage of many swans.

The entertainment was revealed in eight episodes and opened with a chorus of Druids singing 'A Hymn to the Sun'. Then Caractacus and his band of British warriors, played by Ralph Ratcliffe and employees of Cheltenham Gas Works, fought bravely but vainly to repulse the Roman Augustan Legion from Gloucestershire. Episodes two and three provided glimpses of the locality in Saxon and Norman times. Then came the Wars of the Roses. To offset the bloodiness of the conflict, enacted by dozens of Lancastrians and Yorkists (again played by employees of the gas works) trotting about on ingenious hobby horses, episode five depicted rural England during the reign of Elizabeth I. The official souvenir brochure, sixty-four pages with sepia photographs, price 1s, set the scene: 'It is a pretty picture. The old fashioned Maypole dance, the garland dance, a dance by shepherds and shepherdesses, another by milkmaids and ploughboys and finally a parade of two sets of restive hobby horses' (no doubt also played by the guys from the gas works).

In a seventh episode of imaginative dramatic personification, four local rivers, the Thames, Severn, Avon and Chelt, recapped on the action so far and extolled in rhyming couplets the pleasure of being an inland waterway.

On the last day an eager audience once again filled the grandstand at the edge of Pittville Lake. The final episode recaptured the visit of George III with Queen Charlotte and their royal family to Cheltenham in 1788. Bringing the whole gloriously baffling business to an end was a massed march past by the cast singing the National Anthem. From boats in the lake, the choir rendered the 'Eton Boating Song' and 'Home, Sweet Home', and with a final chorus of 'God Save the King' the curtain came down on a show the like of which Cheltenham has never seen before or since.

*　　*　　*

Sgt Maj Wilson of Cheltenham recruiting office with five shop assistants from Cavendish House who joined up together.

When war against Germany was declared on 4 August 1914 Cheltenham, like most towns and cities throughout the country, was gripped by jingoistic euphoria. Recruitment rallies, such as those staged in the Town Hall and the Territorial Army Drill Hall in North Street (to the rear of where Littlewoods now stands), drew eager crowds. Throngs surged to open-air meetings at the Prom end of Clarence Street, and by October 1,400 locals had signed up. Typical of the rhetoric that fired their frenzy were these words, taken from a recruitment officer's speech of the time. 'At home in the past there might have been a good deal of distinction between classes, but in a little ditch called a trench in France, there is only one class – the class that answers to its country's call. In future there will only be two classes among men in this country; the class who went and the class that stayed at home.'

Brisk business was done at the town's first recruitment office in a Great Western Road house under the supervision of Maj Percy Shewell, late of the Indian Staff Corps. One of the first recruits was 33-year-old Edwin Willoughby, editor of the *Gloucestershire Echo*. He was killed a year later, leading his company into action at Gallipoli.

Mr S.J. Gibbons of Boddington Court was appointed the local purchasing officer for cavalry horses, and owners were paid about £50 for each suitable steed received at the repository in Winchcombe Street.

'It'll all be over by Christmas' was a phrase in ready currency in those early weeks of the war. So like lambs to the slaughter they volunteered, young and not so young, rich and poor, clambering to take the king's shilling and see action while there was action to be seen. On the Sunday after war was declared, at a special service in St Matthew's, a bulging congregation, augmented by the mayor, aldermen and town councillors, heard a rousing address from the Revd F.W. Dwelly. They prayed for victory and, as God was undoubtedly on the allies' side, expected it sooner, rather than later.

War brought visible changes to Cheltenham. Montpellier's Rotunda became a club and canteen for volunteers. Fund-raising committees burgeoned to organise dances, concerts, bring-and-buys and at-homes galore, so that within weeks our brave boys at the front had received 70,000 cigarettes, knitted blankets and woollen socks, mufflers and mittens by the cartload.

In November 2,000 soldiers were billeted on local families. Then the population swelled more when Belgian refugees took up residence in relief homes such as St Philip's Lodge in Painswick Road, Western Lodge in Western Road and Oakfield in The Park. The Red Cross established its local headquarters in Montpellier Spa Road and Voluntary Aid Detachment (VAD) hospitals were located at Prestbury Park racecourse, New Court, Lansdown Place, Suffolk Hall in Lypiatt Terrace, Leckhampton Court, Eversleigh in Parabola Road, The Priory in London Road, Gloucester Road School and Naunton Park School. At the latter a plaque can be seen that reads: 'This building was used as a hospital for sick and wounded soldiers during the Great War. It was manned by Gloucestershire Volunteer Aid Detachment no. 106 and was open from 12 June 1915 to 29 December 1918, during which period 2,751 cases were treated.'

The racecourse opened as a 100-bed hospital, receiving its first influx of wounded Belgian soldiers on 28 October 1914. They were treated in the Cheltenham Ward, a room in which more than half a century later punters tippled: it had been renamed the Arkle Bar. A fully equipped operating theatre was located at Prestbury Park, complete with electric lighting installed in June 1914. Belgian, British, Canadian and French casualties from the trenches were ferried by ship to Southampton, then on to Cheltenham aboard special trains. Despite the horrors across the Channel, and despite the parade of wounded and maimed soldiers, fashionable race meetings continued to attract the well-to-do and titled. There was a meet in November 1914, which was probably the first time that many of the recuperating, working-class privates had seen a horse without a cart, and the first time that many of the racegoers had seen suffering.

Reported in the local press was a remark made by a Tommy who spotted an elegant lady sporting a huge, feathery hat: 'The things one sees when one goes without one's gun'.

New Court in Lansdown Place was a private home until it was converted into a hospital at twelve hours' notice in the early weeks of the war. It remained in service until 1919. Leckhampton Court, previously the home of Capt Cecil Elwes, became a VAD hospital in 1915. Today it's the Sue Ryder hospice.

Local schools were keen to make a contribution to the war effort. Pate's Grammar School, Dean Close and Cheltenham College supplied young officers, a high percentage of whom didn't return. And Cheltenham Ladies' College was responsible for St Martin's VAD hospital. This building, now Molloy House in Parabola Road, had been a dormitory but the college converted it for wartime use, and all the nursing staff were former pupils of the school. The Priory, London Road, opened as a hospital in 1916, paid for by public subscription, and Gloucester Road School swapped its desks for beds to become St John's Hospital for the duration.

Between 1914 and 1918 the VAD hospitals received 36,000 war casualties and the town extended its hand to them in various ways. Local firms ran whist drives for the convalescents. Affluent individuals hosted tea parties. And many ordinary families took part in a befriending scheme, inviting a soldier to spend Sunday with them for a taste of normal life and home cooking. The town's VAD hospitals did a fine job. They were well organised and coped with a huge workload efficiently; what's more the standard of care must have been high as only a small percentage of patients failed to recover. Remarkably, all this sterling work was carried out by volunteers, not just the nursing staff, but also those who ran the war hospital supply depot, which was at 28 Imperial Gardens. At least two local volunteer nurses lost their lives by contracting diseases in the course of their duties. Elizabeth Roberts of Hanover Street, St Paul's, was one of these unfortunate women, Anna Shaw of 17 Lypiatt Terrace another.

*　　*　　*

When it wasn't all over by Christmas, when 50,000 British soldiers were killed in October and November 1914 at the first battle of Ypres, when long columns of Cheltonian casualties appeared daily in local newspapers, and when it became obvious that no end to the war was in sight, business at the recruitment offices became less brisk. To spur more local men into uniform, Easter 1915 was designated Recruitment Week. There were open-air meetings all over town, then on Easter Sunday probably the biggest military display ever staged in Cheltenham took place.

Over a mile in length, the procession comprised soldiers on horseback, regimental bands, servicemen cyclists, the Women's Volunteer Reserve, fire brigades, St John's Ambulance and the Red Cross, more military bands, the Gordon Boys Brigade, Church Lads Brigade, Scouts and more bands. Watched by thousands, this drum-beating body

The largest military procession ever seen in town took place on Easter Sunday 1915.

Communiques on the war were posted in the Town Hall.

snaked its way around the town, firing hearts with passionate patriotism as it passed. A few months later, at the battle of Loos, thirty-three Cheltonians were killed on the first day.

Recalling the outbreak of the war some years after it ended, the *Cheltenham Chronicle and Gloucestershire Graphic* noted this curious coincidence. 'The first man of the British Expeditionary Force to land in France on the way to the seat of war was Capt Kenneth Algernon Brook-Murray (OO), RASO and RFO, son of Maj H. Brook-Murray, of Cheltenham. He died of wounds in France two years later. The last to come home was Maj-Gen J.D. McLachlian (OO), who after serving throughout the war was in charge of the British Army of Occupation on the Rhine from 1922 to 1925. He is the son of the late Mr James McLachlian, of Holland House, Cheltenham.'

*   *   *

A famous evacuee who was brought to Cheltenham by the war was Auguste Rodin. As the Germans were marching towards Paris in August 1914 the 74-year-old sculptor thought it was a good time to leave, and was persuaded to come to Cheltenham by his friend Mlle Judith Cladel, who had sisters in the town. The artist enjoyed considerable celebrity in England, and at the time of his arrival an exhibition of his bronzes at a South Kensington museum added to his star status. Nevertheless, the creator of *The Thinker*, *The Kiss* and other noted statues settled in a small Cheltenham hotel named Sussex House and lived simply. A few times each day he walked to the Town Hall where communiques on the progress of the war were posted. In the afternoons he strolled in Pittville Park, or on local hills. Once he visited Tewkesbury. But most to his liking was taking afternoon tea, as Mlle Cladel recalled in an article she wrote for the *Gloucestershire Echo*: 'Then came tea time, at which there were the most dainty niceties for us exiles. Tea is one of the rites of English life which nearly approaches religion. Auguste [Rodin] called it "the symbol of family life". Smiling, he watched with an amused look the amiable movements of the mistress of the house and her daughter who passed out the perfumed beverage and handed round cakes of all sorts in pretty flowered china.'

Datelines

1900	All the town's twenty-eight elementary schools were run by churches. The Assembly Rooms, Cheltenham's main venue for social functions, closed. Population of the town 51,854.
1901	On 22 August Cheltenham's electric tram service began and carried 40,000 fare-paying passengers in its first week.
1902	Prestbury Park hosted its first two-day National Hunt festival. There were riots over the Leckhampton Quarry Company's attempts to close public access to the hill.
1903	Horse-drawn bus services disappeared. The corporation education committee was established. Buffalo Bill's Wild West Show came to town.
1904	Nellie Melba appeared at the Winter Garden. Underground telephone lines were installed.
1905	Tramlines were extended to Leckhampton and Charlton Kings. Cheltenham acquired a new horse-drawn ambulance.
1906	J.E. Sears was elected Liberal MP. The town lamplighter Mr J.W. Austin retired after forty-four years.
1907	The South African war memorial in the Promenade Long Garden was unveiled.
1908	H.H. Martyn & Co. moved to the Sunningend Works, Lansdown.
1909	Foundation stone of St Paul's College chapel in Swindon Road was laid.
1910	Advertisements in the *Echo* offered a cottage and garden at Charlton Kings to let at 1s 9d a week and a six-room house in Church Road, Leckhampton, for sale at £300.
1911	Sandford Mill became a farm. The owner was William Cox, who gave his name to Cox's Meadow.
1912	Thousands watched a flying demonstration by Henri Salmet at Rowlands Field off Old Bath Road.
1913	Gilsmith's Hippodrome in Albion Street opened on 22 September. Jack Judge is said to have written 'It's a long way to Tipperary' in the number-one dressing room, and to have performed the song for the first time on the theatre's stage.
1914	The statue of Edward VII opposite Montpellier Rotunda was unveiled on 10 October.
1915	The wartime Restriction of Lights order prohibited the lighting of public lamps.

1916	Former Cheltenham College pupil Arthur Inglis, a major in the Glosters, became the first man in history to lead tanks into battle. This he did, on foot, at the Battle of Flers Courcelles in the Somme sector. Remarkably Inglis survived this action, but in 1918 was injured by shell fragments and died from these wounds in 1919 at the age of thirty-four. He is buried in Prestbury churchyard.
1917	Women porters were employed by the Midland Railway Company.
1918	On 11 November special editions of the *Echo* appeared with the message: 'The armistice was signed at five o'clock this morning. The star of peace returns.'
1919	A 115-acre site off Gloucester Road was bought by the corporation to be developed as the St Marks estate.

FOUR

Between the Wars 1920–39

W hen the guns of the First World War fell silent on 11 November 1918, almost every parish in the country set about raising a plaque to local heroes who had not returned. Holy Trinity in Portland Street is believed to have been the first Cheltenham church to erect a memorial tablet, but examples can be found in many of the town's places of worship. Bishops Cleeve was one of the first surrounding villages to have a stone cross to the fallen, which was unveiled in September 1919.

In December of that year a committee under the chairmanship of Cheltenham's Mayor, Alderman J.D. Bendall, was charged with the task of finding a site, sourcing a design, funding and building a memorial in the town. The committee made its requirements known and suggestions aplenty were received. One was for a hydropathic clinic to be built for the use of invalided servicemen and others. Another envisaged a new outpatients' department for the general hospital. The installation of a pipe organ in the Town Hall, complemented by a wall plaque and pair of captured German field guns came under consideration. And a further proposal was to move the brace of Russian cannons captured during the Crimean War from outside the Queen's Hotel and replace them with a new memorial.

Most imaginative of all was a mooted scheme to demolish five buildings on the west side of Well Walk, thus opening a clear view of St Mary's parish church. This idea would have changed the appearance of the town centre considerably, probably for the better, but it was not to be.

Although it still had no idea what Cheltenham's memorial would be, the committee at least secured a suitable site. Plans to erect a bandstand in the Promenade Long Garden were shelved and instead it was decided that the spot would be used for . . . whatever was eventually chosen. In spring 1920 the matter was still being discussed.

A constable keeps a keen eye on the postwar Prom.

The committee invited the submission of designs for a memorial and thirty-five sets of plans were put forward. This number was whittled down to four. The first came from Col J.C. Griffith JP, who described his idea for a replica of Rome's Temple of Vesta in these words: 'The little temple, with columns of rich creamy golden stone, with its russet red-tiled roof, a work of exquisite grace of the purest period of classical art, in harmony with the architecture of the surrounding buildings, would under the shadow of trees be an object of rare beauty in our Promenade.' The suggestion was dismissed. Next was a design by H.H. Martyn. The local firm's sculptor, Robert Lindsay Clark, captured something of the torment of the First World War in his statue *The broken limber* (a limber, by the way, is the detachable front part of a horse-drawn gun carriage), which depicted a lifesize Royal Horse Artillery team and driver struggling over a shell-torn battlefield. The suggestion was again dismissed, but small castings of the Lindsay Clark creation can be seen in Cheltenham's Clarence Street museum and the Imperial War Museum, Lambeth, London. No record of the third design exists, as it was destroyed in a fire at the Municipal Offices in the 1960s.

The execution chosen by the committee was by R.L. Boulton & Sons, of Bath Road, the local firm of stonemasons that had already made numerous memorials for towns and villages across the country. Boulton's concept was a gold-topped cenotaph on a stone base in black marble, or red Scot's granite, covered by a canopy supported on four classical pillars, estimated price £3,500. An appeal was launched to raise the funds, but by September 1920 only £1,150 had been collected. Boulton's was asked by the cap-in-hand committee for a budget-priced version of the original and the result is the 24ft high simple cenotaph that stands in the Prom today. It cost £2,100 to build and inscribe the memorial, which was paid for by public subscription and a grant of £400 from the Cheltenham prisoner of war fund.

After all the indecision and embarrassment Cheltenham's war memorial was finally unveiled on 1 October 1921. Presiding at the ceremony was Gen Sir Robert Fanshawe,

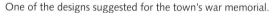

One of the designs suggested for the town's war memorial.

commander of the old 48th Division in which many local men had served. The huge crowd that filled the Prom comprised relatives of the fallen, ex-service personnel, regular and territorial soldiers, civic and other dignities – and a group of 250 children whose fathers had not returned from the trenches. The inscription on the memorial was supplied by the Very Revd Reginald Waterfield, Dean of Hereford and former principal of Cheltenham College. It reads:

> Remember the men of Cheltenham who gave their lives for you in the Great War of 1914–1919. If they were Strangers to one another here in their common home, they served and wrought and died in many lands near and far as a Band of Brothers. Learn from them so to live and die that, when you have followed them and are no more seen, you may, like them, be remembered and regretted.

*   *   *

With peace came a virtual end to military orders for aeroplanes at the Sunningend Works that the Gloucestershire Aircraft Company shared with H.H. Martyn & Co. To remain in business the company had to display its wares to a worldwide audience and it set out to attract global attention by producing fast, well-engineered aeroplanes. The brilliant Harry Folland, internationally regarded for designing racing planes, was

Gloster VI Golden Arrow designed by Harry Folland for the 1926 Schneider Trophy race.

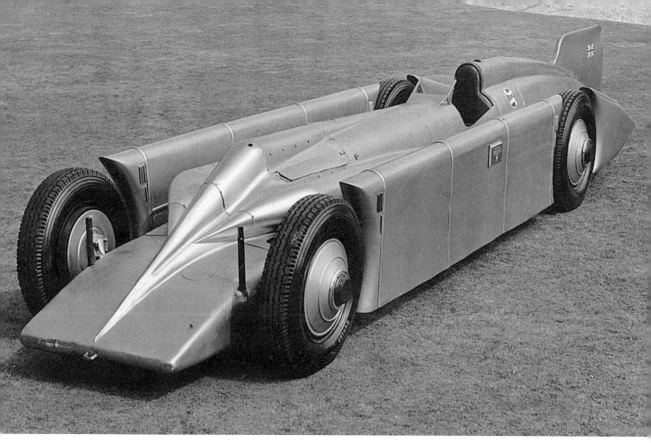

H.H. Martyn made parts of Henry Seagrave's world land-speed record-breaking car Golden Arrow.

engaged as chief engineer in 1921. Under his direction the Mars-1 Bamel biplane was conceived, built and flown in under four weeks and won the Aerial Derby, clocking 163.3mph with test pilot J.H. James at the controls. The plane won the same event for the next two years and set a British air speed record of 196.4mph.

The most prestigious air race of the age was the Schneider Trophy, for which sea planes competed over a measured triangular course. Folland produced a series of designs intended to capture the trophy for the Cheltenham firm, but the Napier engines used let the side down time and again. In a straight line the GAC entries were difficult to catch and the firm established a world speed record for a float biplane of 277.1mph at the Venice Schneider Trophy race in 1927. But when banking sharply into a turn the Napier engines had a tendency to splutter and die. Even with this serious handicap the company's entry came second in the event at Baltimore in 1925.

As the name of the firm changed from 'Gloucestershire' to 'Gloster' a year later, Harry Folland's design for the last ever Schneider Trophy at Calshot in 1929 was dubbed the Gloster VI Golden Arrow. It was his first monoplane and an undisputed masterpiece. An aviation publication of the time reported: 'It seems more the conception of an artist who can make and create his own lines by the stroke of a brush, than the work of a designer who is bounded by the principles of engineering.' Despite its breathtaking lines, engine trouble dogged Folland's finest and Gloster withdrew from the race.

By the mid-1920s new orders from the Air Ministry in Britain and from customers overseas had been received, which meant production at Cheltenham was bursting at the seams. For years the company had tested planes at Hucclecote, towing them for trials behind a lorry. (Drivers were instructed to make an official stop at the Oddfellows Arms on the Shurdington Road to let the landing-gear wheel bearings cool down.) In 1925 GAC bought the 200-acre Hucclecote site for £15,000, and by the end of the decade production of aircraft had moved there from Cheltenham.

*   *   *

H.H. Martyn remained one of the largest employers in the town and, as ever, was involved in projects that demanded the excellent craftsmanship for which the firm was renowned. Golden Arrow – the monster car in which Sir Henry Segrave captured the world land-speed record in 1929 – was one of them. Segrave commissioned the firm to construct the sponsons that ran between the vehicle's front and back wheels. Before a record-breaking run these were packed with ice to cool the 930hp engine. After the run this ice had turned to boiling water.

In the 1920s Wolseley motor cars were made on a sub-contract basis at Sunningend. Martyn's also designed and built a motor scooter called the Unibus, which was way ahead of its time from an engineering aspect, but at 90 guineas was way out of the price range of its market.

Besides building planes, cars and fitting out ocean liners, Martyn's continued to produce fine art and craft work, as well as fulfilling its engineering contracts. During the 1920s Martyn's produced 75 per cent of all statues, ornamental screening, decorative doors, gates and similar art metalwork ordered in Britain.

*   *   *

Cheltenham's reputation as a shopping mecca (early closing Wednesdays and Saturdays) was well established by the 1920s, with prestigious department stores such as Cavendish House, Shirers and E.L. Ward's (where Littlewoods is now).

After a major rebuild and refurbishment in 1923 E.L. Ward advertised that 'The opening of our commodious premises situated in the heart of Cheltenham's shopping centre . . . marks another milestone of progress in the history of this extensive store'. The shop was certainly extensive – and in parts decidedly non-PC by today's standards. You could, for example, pop along to the Furs Department and find red fox ties at 35s 9d, a handsome seal coat with cuffs of beaver for 10 guineas, or a lady's Jaquard coat in mole at 45s 9d. Other departments included Umbrellas and Handbags (in leather,

The New Sensation . .

sweeping across the hat horizon, made by Walmar—Britain's lightweight specialists.

Entirely hand made, the careless air of Jaunty felts is never carelessly achieved.

There is a style to suit every head, and all are made in the famous Walmar fittings, 6⅝ to 7½.

All one price . . . 12/9

Walmar Hat

INDY RIDGE. The loosely tucked crown combined with the snap brim, provides an ideal lightweight fur felt Hat for the sportsman. Fine petersham ribbon is used for the trimming.

a Walmar Hat

BROOMSTAGES. Adapted for town or sports wear, this charming Hat has the new square crown and a long pointed brim, with a bandeau fitting back. It is trimmed with contrast petersham, and is made in lightweight fur felt.

Sketched from our Coat Dept.

A useful Coat for early Autumn wear. Made in REAL WESTMORLAND TWEED—pure wool— a cloth that tells its own story. Delightful Heather Mixtures of Green, Blues, Browns, Greys   35/9

Plain tailor-made Costume to match   45/9

a Walmar Hat

DAMABOUT. The squarish crown with the two slouch tucks is the attractive feature of this fur felt. The petersham trimming with the felt ends in front give a small wing effect.

E. L. WARD LTD.
The Modern Store :: Cheltenham

a Walmar Hat

GREENGATES. The attractiveness of this sports felt is enhanced by the lightly tucked crown, and self coloured eyelets, it has a snap brim, and is trimmed with a band and tailored bow of petersham. All leading shades.

suede, crocodile and Morocco), Fancy Goods, Drapery, Corsetry, Gloves, Hosiery and Lace. In the Millinery department of 1923 an extravagant confection of a hat – 'a charming Paris model in black panne velvet, edged with lace and paradise plume' – could be yours for 45*s* 11*d*. In Blouses and Sports Coats on the first floor 'Ladies' ice wool wraps, suitable for motoring' were offered at 6*s* 11*d*.

In 1926 Dunn's, the men's hat retailer, occupied a landmark building on the corner of the High Street and Winchcombe Street. The half timbered, Swiss chalet-style shop featured a carved frieze over the window, the top section of which was in stained glass.

Banks

Imperial Art Gallery

RICHARD KITCHIN

STUDIED: SLADE SCHOOL OF ART, LONDON
           FINE ARTS ACADEMY, FLORENCE,
           ITALY
           GRANDE CHAUMIÈRE, PARIS

MAJOR COMMISSIONS

LT. GEN. SIR CHARLES KAVANAGH
THE DUCHESS OF LEINSTER
VISCOUNT & VISCOUNTESS LYMINGTON
LADY IRIS MOUNTBATTEN
& NUMEROUS OTHERS

COMMISSIONS NOW ACCEPTED

THE PROMENADE, CHELTENHAM
Telephone 22328

Banks was a well-known Cheltenham retailer for many years and occupied the shop that is now Waterstones. There's a story that in the 1920s, when the Promenade was considered strictly a no-go area for the hoi polloi, the prosperous owner of Banks raised his hat to a minor-titled (and probably impecunious) lady customer on his way to work. In the following morning's post he received a letter of sharp rebuke from Madam, who made it quite clear that she did not wish to be acknowledged in public by a mere tradesman.

Cheltenham's Promenade was the town's showpiece and for the fashion conscious it was the place to see and be seen. Many of them spent at least the best part of one day a week at Foice's. The ordinary had haircuts; the discerning went to Foice's. At least that was how Cheltenham's most up-market crimper billed itself. According to an advert from the 1920s this was no mere hairdresser's, but 'a series of charming salons in which artists express their art'. There was even poetry in the words on Foice's shop front: 'Coiffeurs. Posticheurs. Massage and manicure. Pedicure and chiropody.' (Posticheurs meant they made wigs.) And what a shop front – Art Nouveau curvaceous, turned hardwood framed, black marble base. Gorgeous. Mr F.J. Foice, a member of the International Hairdressing Academy of London, left Kensington for Cheltenham in 1901. In July of that year he acquired premises at 20 The Promenade, which had previously been occupied by a tailoring business. A major refurbishment marked the firm's twenty-fifth anniversary, by which time Foice & Co. employed a staff of twenty-five in the salon.

Clients were often serenaded into 20 The Prom by the Spa Harp Trio. A feature of Cheltenham town centre from the 1920s to the '50s, this group of buskers played harp, cornet and flute from a pitch outside Foice's and another in Montpellier Walk. Foice's brochure of 1926 pointed out: 'We are rather proud of the fact that customers who came to us as children are still patrons and many return after years of absence in India and the Colonies.' On the ground floor the ladies' department was reached via a lounge complete with divans and aspidistras. Beyond this oasis of tranquillity were individual salons, partitioned in mahogany and opaque glass, designed to keep prying eyes off Foice's artists at work. This was probably just as well, given that the list of treatments available in 1926 included not only cutting, bobbing, shingling, singeing, waving, shampooing and manicure, but also violet ray, high frequency ray, coloured ray, vibratory massage, hand massage, the gas curling lamp – and the mysterious Hairometer.

No customer ever suffered from cold feet in Foice's, thanks to 'A convenient type of foot rest, the mat on which conceals a foot warmer which is heated from the central heating system'. They thought of everything. Even if you were bald as a coot, Foice's was the hairdresser for you. Up on the top floor was the postiche department, where up to forty women workers at a time strained their eyes making wigs from human hair.

*   *   *

Gradually increasing affluence and leisure time enabled new industries to spring up. Caravan making was a thriving industry in Cheltenham of the 1920s, with at least three manufacturers working in the town. Adams Caravans Ltd operated from Copt Elm Road, Charlton Kings. Old Bath Road was the business address of Siddall Caravans. But the firm that gained a national reputation for the craftsmanship quality of its travelling homes was the Cheltenham Caravan Company Ltd. One of the oldest caravan makers in Britain, the company was founded by a Mr Gardner in Buckinghamshire just after the First World War. In 1922 the business transferred to Cheltenham where a factory was established in Leckhampton Road. The site had previously been a stone yard for the quarry on the hill, and is now the Leckhampton Industrial Estate.

Business boomed. Army surplus materials were in abundant supply and were ideal for caravan making. Cheltenham had a ready pool of skilled labour. Inexpensive cars such as the Austin Seven gave an ever growing number of people the freedom of the road, and taking a caravan in tow meant a holiday anywhere, any time. Caravan making remained an important employer in the town for the next half century.

*   *   *

Whatever your choice for your new Spring Outfit—be it Swaggers or Suits—GOUGH & EDWARDS have the Smartest at the Lowest Prices. . . .

Attractive New Suit with new style Swagger to match. (on right) **59/6**

Smart 2-piece Suit in new lightweight tweeds. **49/11**

In our Millinery Department you will find a marvellous collection of Hats in all the newest styles.

GOUGH
AND EDWARDS,
'phone—CHELTENHAM—3604

To make your ensemble complete, your Gloves and Hosiery must be just "right." We only stock the best known and most reliable makes.

Various attempts to boost the town's tourist trade were made between the wars. The Chamber of Commerce sponsored a British Gaumont-made travelogue about the town, silent of course, which was shown as a support film to major features in cinemas around the country.

Time and again the town council attempted to rekindle long gone interest in the virtues of Cheltenham as a fashionable spa, but these efforts met with limited success. In 1932 a new campaign of advertisements was launched inviting local people to avail themselves of the spa with the slogan 'The cure at your door'. Curiously the treatments on offer then seem remarkably up to date now. There's the ultra violet ray, a sun bed by another name. There's the aerated whirlpool, or jacuzzi as we now say. There's the Vichy and scotch douche, that's a power shower to you and me. And there's the plombieres, a device for colonic irrigation (terribly popular with today's feng shui set). There was, incidentally, also something called the 'Schnee four cell treatment', a hydro-electric bath, which must have been an early type of jacuzzi.

However, visitors did begin to arrive in increasing numbers during the inter-war years, as the town established itself as a conference centre. In 1931 alone the Town Hall hosted annual gatherings of goldsmiths, sales managers, the International Brotherhood of Magicians, the Co-op Guild, Library Association, plus the Midland Cat Show and the first Open Dog Show of the Ladies' Kennel Society.

*   *   *

For those with the luxury of leisure in 1920s Cheltenham, cafés were places in which to linger, meet friends, chat and watch the world go by. So when the Gloucestershire Dairy opened a roof garden above its Promenade Café in 1928, the conservatory-like venue (still in use as a hairdressers) was advertised as 'making a fascinating resort, where the life of the Promenade may be viewed in comfort and the daintiest of meals can be enjoyed'.

Cadena Cafés – there was one in the High Street and another on the corner of the Prom and Imperial Lane – were popular too, where mob-capped, black-frocked, frilly-pinnied waitresses fetched and carried.

'The largest and highest class contracting purveyors and caterers' was how George's of Cheltenham described itself. Founded in 1800 by a pastry cook and confectioner named David George, the firm remained a local institution for 140 years. George's Model Bakery occupied the building in Clarence Street that today stands adjacent to the art gallery and museum. There were other premises in town at 18 Montpellier Walk, Charlton Kings, Pittville, and the most grand of all a shop and restaurant at 365–7 High Street, where W.H. Smith now resides. It was in the latter, in 1922, that the company opened its new tea room on the first floor, a palm court of a place with pristine linen table cloths, white china crockery, Chinese patterned wallpaper and elegant appointments.

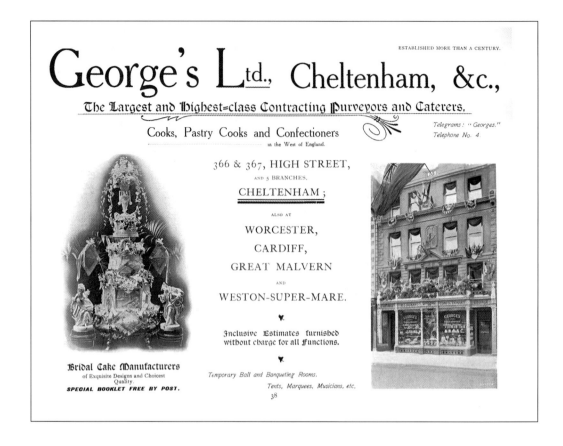

After church on a Sunday, the well-to-do looked for other amusement and from 3 May 1920 onwards found it in Imperial Gardens, where an impressive – and at £1,850 highly expensive – pagoda-shaped bandstand was unveiled. Between the wars, uniformed bands entertained, when well-heeled shoes tapped to the tunes being played from the pagoda. You can still see the bandstand, but you have to go to Bognor for the privilege. Cheltenham sold it to the south-coast town in 1948 for a mere £175.

When it was opened in 1927 Sandford Park was described as having 'a good collection of ornamental trees and shrubs, including varieties of pyrus, maples, barberries and cotoneasters, also a handsome specimen of a weeping willow, a Tree of Heaven and a group of Judas trees'. The area of Sandford Park that abuts the High Street was laid out as a formal Italian garden. Behind it was a water feature, a man-made brook plumbed from the Chelt to tumble over rustic rocks. Two years after the park opened the arched, ornate drinking fountain, which can be seen to this day at the Keynsham Road entrance, was installed. It originally stood at Westal Green.

* * *

The worldwide depression of the 1930s didn't bypass the town, and needless to say the section of society that was hardest hit was the one that could afford it least. 'Overshadowing everything is the dark cloud of unemployment,' reported the *Gloucestershire Chronicle*. The population of the borough was around 50,000 with one in five people out of work. One of the few places where business was brisk was the Salvation Army soup kitchen in New Street, where 400 penny meals were served a day.

Stringent cutbacks exacerbated the problem of unemployment. Forced to reduce spending by £8,000, the education committee shelved plans for new schools in Cheltenham, Bourton and Tewkesbury. It did, however, raise the school leaving age from fourteen to fifteen. Also discarded was the proposal to turn the open-air Alstone Baths into a lido, and even the winter season of Town Hall concerts was shortened by nine weeks to save paying musicians in the municipal orchestra.

The clearance of slums, such as back-to-backs in Swindon Passage, Stanhope Street and St Pauls, necessitated new housing, and precious jobs were created at building sites in Whaddon, St Marks, Pates Avenue and the Moors estate. Other pockets of appalling housing were razed at this time too. Between Painswick Road and Great Norwood Street is a service lane named Casino Place. Until they were demolished in the 1930s, some eighteen back-to-back houses were tucked into this narrow space. The curious name, incidentally, was taken from Casino House, described as 'a very elegant villa with 14 rooms', which was built in 1824, then demolished in the 1930s to make way for 2 to 12 Painswick Road. All that remains of the grand pile today is the brick boundary wall and a stone pier on the corner of St James's Place. The slum clearance was well intentioned, but with hindsight it's easy to see that the way in which the programme was implemented merely stored up problems for the future. People from old run-down ghettos were moved *en masse* to newly built ones. The shared sub-culture of social deprivation was exactly the same, only now they didn't have to share a lavatory with everyone else in the street.

*   *   *

With depression at home and war clouds gathering over Europe, the national and local press welcomed with open arms the unfolding story of a juicy murder mystery for which Cheltenham provided the location.

The gruesome business started with an anticlimax, when a pathologist's report declared that blood found at Haw bridge in January 1938 was not human. Three weeks later fishermen Jack Duffield, Edgar Bevan and Sidney Church, working a stretch of the Severn downstream from Haw, netted an unexpected catch – the torso of an adult man, headless and limbless. New tests revealed that the blood on the bridge was, after all, human and the stage was set for a shock-horror drama that captured the country's attention.

A macabre tale unfolded when bloodstains were discovered on Haw bridge.

Celebrated Home Office pathologist Sir Bernard Spilsbury arrived to examine the remains and dispatched organs to his London laboratory. Assigned to the case were Detective Inspector Percy Worth and Detective Sergeant James Shewry of Scotland Yard, who appeared at the scene of the incident in bowler hats and Crombie overcoats – *de rigueur* in Westminster, incongruous in Tirley. Journalists from every national paper mingled with a crowd of 5,000 at Haw bridge, hoping dragging operations on the river would bring more gore to the surface. And they did. First an arm. Then a leg. Followed by another arm. The hands and feet had been severed. Enough of the body was now assembled to issue a limited description of the deceased. The dead man was in his mid-fifties, about 5ft 9in tall and weighing around 11 stone.

The next chapter of the story started routinely when police received a call from the owner of Cheltenham's Regent Garage to say that a blue Daimler saloon left at the premises a month earlier on 4 January had not been collected. Ownership of the car was traced to Capt William Bernard Butt of Old Bath Road, Leckhampton, where officers heard from Butt's invalid wife Edith and the live-in nurse who looked after her, Mrs Irene Sullivan, that William Butt had not been seen by them since the day the Daimler was left at Regent Garage. Capt Butt's description? He was in his mid-fifties, about 5ft 9in tall and weighed around 11 stone.

Among the missing man's possessions were found letters from Brian Sullivan, whose mother was Mrs Butt's nurse. At a news conference these letters were said to suggest that Brian Sullivan and William Butt 'were on exceptionally friendly terms and that they often visited Tower Lodge [on Leckhampton Hill] together'. Tower Lodge – rented by the Sullivans – had recently been in the news. On 24 January Mrs Sullivan had discovered her 27-year-old son Brian there, dead. He was in his bedroom, the gas pipe was cut and gaps around the door and windows were sealed. Crowds now gathered on

Dragging operations netted severed human limbs.

The victim – Capt William Bernard Butt.

Gigolo Brian Sullivan was found dead at Tower Lodge.

Crowds gathered as the grisly finds were uncovered.

the hill, as the small gothic lodge with its castellated roof became the focus of attention in the increasingly macabre affair. Beneath the flagstone floor police unearthed a heavily bloodstained overcoat belonging to Capt Butt. An axe with unidentified stains was removed from the lodge. And among Brian Sullivan's belongings were the keys to Butt's Daimler.

As the date of the Haw Bridge torso inquest loomed, efforts to find the missing head were redoubled. A police appeal brought forward members of the public who helped search Leckhampton quarries, Cranham Woods and every vacant property within a 15-mile radius, but no head was discovered. In those pre-DNA days it was, therefore, a foregone conclusion that Coroner Mr R.D. Lane was forced to accept 'The jury are unanimous on an open verdict on the body of an unidentified male person and as to the cause of death'. Sir Bernard Spilsbury did, however, report that excessive bruising in the lumbar region of the torso was consistent with being hit from behind by a fast-moving car.

Although the mystery was intact, the drama was at an end. National newspapers returned to speculation of when Hitler would spark war in Europe. Locally there was the opening of a new golf club house on Cleeve Hill and a beautiful baby competition at Ward's department store to occupy the pages of the *Gloucestershire Graphic*.

Messrs Spilsbury, Worth and Shewry returned to the capital. Capt Butt's wife went to live with relatives in Aston on Carrant. And Irene Sullivan successfully sued a journalist who'd implicated her in evil dealings at Tower Lodge, was paid handsomely for her 'I tell all' story in the *Empire News* and left Cheltenham for the anonymity of London.

That's the bones of the story, but what really happened? It appears that the goings on at Tower Lodge were a talking point in Leckhampton for all the time, in the 1930s, that Brian Sullivan and his mother rented the place. Brian was employed as a professional dance partner at the Piccadilly Hotel in London where he came into contact with the bright young things and glitterati of the time. Besides the quick step and tango, Brian offered a nifty line in arranging illegal abortions, which – so reports of the time suggested – were carried out by his mother at weekends in Tower Lodge. William Butt and Brian were lovers, but when the affair turned sour the captain threatened to tell of the Sullivans' unsavoury service, unless – perhaps – he was paid to keep quiet. Instead of paying him off, the Sullivans arranged to see him off, permanently. His body was dismembered by Irene Sullivan, so reports of the time alleged, and the head and hands disposed of thoroughly so as to make positive identification, and therefore incrimination of the Sullivans, impossible.

Most baffling of all is Brian Sullivan's suicide – if that's what it was. Did he take his own life because he was afraid his part in the coterie of wickedness might be revealed? Probably not. Brian's post mortem established that he died *after* the pathologist declared the blood on Haw bridge was not human – and *before* the torso was netted by the Severn fishermen. So when he died Brian Sullivan had every reason to believe he was in the clear. The room in which he died had been carefully prepared – or staged? –

Faces at the inquest, which returned an open verdict.

to make his death look like *felo de se*. There was a gas tap in the room, but instead of simply turning this on, which could have been interpreted as an accident, the pipe leading to the tap had been cut.

In the late 1970s a police officer who'd worked on the case, a local journalist who was closely involved in reporting the story, and a number of people who knew the Sullivans revealed that they were unanimous in one belief. When Mrs Sullivan's account of events appeared in the *Empire News* under the headline 'I tell all', she didn't.

*   *   *

Cheltenham was destined to become the hub of long-distance road-passenger transport when Mr G. Readings founded Black and White Motorways in the town in 1926. Visiting the town the entrepreneur recognised an opportunity, as he told a *Gloucestershire Chronicle* reporter: 'it struck me at the time rather poorly served in the matter of long distance services, a very likely spot for touring, and a suitable distance from London for a road service.' The firm began with three motor coaches and at first simply offered tours of the town. But when a Cheltenham to London service was introduced the idea caught on. Within a year of start-up the Black and White fleet had swollen to eleven coaches and three daily services to the capital were operating. By 1928 twenty-one vehicles were being run to more and more destinations – Malvern, Worcester, Hereford and beyond – and the firm became a limited company with a capital of £7,000. The expansion continued apace until by the end of the decade Black and White Motorways Ltd was the largest long-distance coach operator in the country, with a fleet of forty coaches providing services to all parts of the country. The fleet included eighteen Leyland Tigers. Costing £1,700 each, these offered Concorde-class luxury at the time. Carpets, curtains, reading lamps, specimen vases, an on-board lavatory, blue leather and moquette upholstery – and a coach host or hostess to serve drinks.

Long-distance travellers were served by the Black and White coach station in St Margaret's Road, which placed Cheltenham at the centre of the national road network. During the 1920s the number of coach passengers passing through the town increased from 350,000 to 3 million.

*   *   *

The town's most impressive railway station was St James's, which stood in the square of the same name. It was from this terminus station with its cobbled approach and impressive portico that the famous Cheltenham Flyer began its journey to the capital. For many years this was the flagship (or flag train) of the GWR. It was written about in *The Times*, cartooned in *Punch*, a biography of the train was published in 1934, and there was even a song entitled (no cigars for guessing) 'The Cheltenham Flyer'.

BLACK & WHITE
MOTORWAYS LTD.

CHELTENHAM SPA
TELEPHONE 3067

RECULAR LUXURY COACH SERVICES TO CHELTENHAM SPA FROM LONDON
& ALL PARTS OF THE MIDLANDS. SOUTH COAST & SOUTH WALES
LUXURY TOURS OF THE COTSWOLDS. WYE VALLEY & FOREST OF DEAN
SHAKESPEARE COUNTRY ETC

Purists insist that the train wasn't actually called the 'Cheltenham Flyer' and strictly speaking they're right. The word 'Flyer' appeared on the train's nameplate, but its official title was the 'Cheltenham Spa Express'. To add to the confusion, the train was officially only called the 'Flyer', or 'Spa Express' from Swindon to London. Another curiosity is that the names 'Cheltenham Flyer', or 'Cheltenham Spa Express' referred not to a locomotive, but to the whole train. Various Castle class engines pulled the train, the fastest ever to do so being no. 5006 *Tregenna Castle*. On 6 June 1932 the train completed the 77¼ miles along 'Brunel's billiard board' from Swindon to London in 56 minutes and 47 seconds at an average speed of 81.6mph. The nameplate of the fastest train in the world, as the 'Cheltenham Flyer' was billed, can be seen today at the National Railway Museum, York.

*   *   *

In January 1937 a traffic census was taken in Cheltenham's High Street. The total number of road users passing both ways (no one-way system then) was counted between the hours of 6 a.m. and 10 p.m., and the findings were cars 6,869, bicycles 7,408, horses 174. It's the number of horses that comes as a surprise, isn't it? We mistakenly think that horses disappeared from our streets when the internal combustion engine made its noisy entrance. But in fact many delivery vehicles were powered by four legs well into the 1960s. Until then the Gloucestershire Dairy had horse-drawn milk floats. Coal merchants arrived with your order of Phurnacite or coke cobbles on a wagon pulled by Dobbin. And the rag and bone man's incomprehensible cry accompanied the clop of a piebald pony, nonchalantly chomping from a nose bag.

The Strand became the town's first one-way street. Boot's roundabout appeared. The first Belisha beacon pedestrian crossing crossed St Margaret's Road, and Cheltenham's first traffic lights were installed at the junction of Bath Road and Suffolk Road.

The acquisition of a motorised Leyland fire appliance in 1923 made the local service more of a force to be reckoned with. On 11 October that year members of the town council and the rural district council gathered in Pittville Park for a demonstration of the state-of-the-art Leyland fire engine. Firstly a representative of the company proved the power of its pump by shooting a jet of water clean over the Pump Room's rotunda. Next, seven hoses were squirted simultaneously. Then, to clinch the deal, the mayor and selected councillors were given a ride on the fire engine at high speed round the park.

*   *   *

Local composer Gustav Holst conducted his newly penned 'Choral Fantasia' at the 1930 Three Choirs Festival in Gloucester Cathedral. 'It was not at first hearing even moderately inspiring,' concluded a local critic.

'Aerated, purified and maintained at an average temperature of 70 degrees – the finest "Lido" in the West of England,' reads a town guide of the day.

North Street cinema became a repertory theatre, while Highbury Congregational church in Winchcombe Street was razed to make way for the Gaumont Palace (now Odeon). 'Half a million bricks, 300 tons of steel – and all of it British – will be used in building Cheltenham's new super-cinema,' enthused the *Chronicle*. Two other cinemas appeared. The ABC Regal was built in the Prom on the site of the Imperial Spa, and the Essoldo brought silver-screen glamour to the Lower High Street.

Crowds flocked to Parton Farm, Churchdown, to see Sir Alan Cobham's Flying Circus. 'Capt Price with superb abandon flung himself out of a plane rocketing 2,000 feet above the earth. His parachute fluttered and filled and with fine judgment he drifted down to the safety of the flying field,' read the report.

The Lido was built at a cost of £15,700 on corporation allotments, but thousands of local bathers preferred to swim in the Severn at Wainlodes on sunny, summer weekends.

Motor rodeos at the Athletic Ground in Albion Street attracted crowds of 8,000, and many local people enjoyed the novelty of a free stroll for the first time in Montpellier Gardens when entrance charges were dropped (though you still had to pay to enter Pittville Park).

Motor rodeos at the Athletic ground in Albion Street attracted large crowds.

Chapman's Circus came to town in 1935. Three elephants advertising the fact were padding along Albion Street when – passing Bloodworth's corn merchants – they caught a whiff of tasty morsels. Entering the shop, the jumbo trio scoffed a good deal of stock, especially the dog biscuits.

In May of the same year Cheltenham's streets were bedecked with bunting for the silver jubilee of George V and Queen Mary. To mark the royal beano, beacons were lit on Leckhampton Hill. Another right royal day was had on Wednesday 12 May 1937. 'Today the Coronation of their most gracious majesties King George VI and Queen Elizabeth is being celebrated throughout the British Empire with joyous enthusiasm. But nowhere will the joy be greater than in Cheltenham, proud of its devotion to the throne.' This paragraph opened the official souvenir programme (price 3*d*) of the town's coronation day celebrations. This unexpected event, brought about by the abdication of Edward VIII, was just the tonic people needed. Flags fluttered above the numerous street parties staged in town. Shops and businesses brandished bunting. There were entertainments and music, a carnival procession from Montpellier with elaborate floats galore and, to top the lot, the sun shone.

Photo: *Debenhams, Longman & Co. Ltd.*

CHELTENHAM'S CORONATION MAYOR AND MAYORESS
(Councillor D. L. LIPSON, M.A., J.P., and Mrs. LIPSON)

MAYOR'S PARLOUR.

Foreword.   May 12th 1931

   To-day the Coronation of their Most Gracious
Majesties King George VI & Queen Elizabeth
is being celebrated throughout the British
Empire with joyous enthusiasm, but nowhere
will the joy be greater than in Cheltenham,
proud of its devotion to the Throne.
   To-day we pray that their Majesties may
have a long & glorious reign, over a people
happy & contented & an Empire rejoicing in
Peace & Prosperity, in a World where Good Will
shall prevail.
   God bless their Majesties!

                                    Daniel L. Lipson.
                                    Mayor.

From early morning the bells of St Mary's parish church in town rang out. Then the grand opening ceremony unfolded at the Winter Garden. Cheltenham's loyalty to the crown was affirmed by the mayor, Councillor D.L. Lipson, and a programme of music by Edward Elgar, Edward German, Arthur Sullivan and other British composers was performed by the 12th Royal Lancers. At the athletic ground in Albion Street a grand open-air variety show was staged – admission free, or 1s for a seat in the main stand. Performers on the bill included 'The Victas – inimitable athletes in their unique barrel jumping act', and 'Les Beaucaires – the funniest juggling act in Vaudeville'. There was more hilarity to follow. 'Fratelli – the comedy table leaping trick cyclist', preceded 'Hiker and Hike – in a comedy hiking speciality act'. Then rounding off the entertainment came 'Swan and Leigh – the comedy horizontal bar gymnasts in their sensational looping act'. Back at the pavilion in Montpellier Gardens 'Chick Fowler's Coronation Revellers in a collaboration of coronation concoctions' was packing 'em in. Chick Fowler hailed from the Forest of Dean and achieved celebrity as a wireless comedian with his 'Gloucestershire George' monologues (a West Country version of Stanley Holloway) heard regularly during the '30s on BBC Midlands variety shows.

Children were not forgotten in all the merrymaking. Throughout the day Punch and Judy shows were given at recreation grounds around the town by puppeteer Mr H. Hewett, who performed from the back of a specially converted lorry. At 6 p.m. the coronation carnival procession set off from the top of Montpellier. Afterwards anyone with energy still to burn just had time to dash home and change into their best bib and tucker for the 'Non stop coronation carnival ball', 9 p.m. to 3 a.m. Music for this Town Hall extravaganza was provided by The Ambassadors Dance Band and tickets were 3s 6d. The price was a bit steep, but then it was a special occasion.

*   *   *

Gloucestershire's cricket team of the '30s included the all-time great Wally Hammond, whose presence in the team overshadowed the considerable talents of Cheltenham-born Charles Barnett. Both were test players. Charles Barnett was born in Cheltenham in 1910 and first played for Gloucestershire in 1927 while a pupil at Wycliffe College. He turned professional in 1929, usually batting at number five and regularly scored 2,000 runs a season. Barnett played for England in twenty tests. The first women's cricket match played locally was at Cheltenham's Victoria Ground in 1936.

National Hunt meetings at Prestbury Park – where the Totaliser was installed in 1930 – were dominated by Golden Miller, the wonder horse that won the Gold Cup five times in succession. Cheltenham jockey Tim Hamey won the Grand National on Forbra in 1932, while another local rider, William Stott, was champion jockey over the sticks five years in a row.

The Robins enjoyed moderate success in the Birmingham Combination senior league with George Blackburn, a former Mansfield player, as coach.

In water polo the town regularly topped the Western Counties senior league and two town team members – Maurice Turk and J.J. Voyce – played for England.

The West of England Grand National, one of greyhound racing's leading events, was run at the newly built Cheltenham and Gloucester stadium in Longlevens and boxing matches were staged regularly at the Winter Garden.

Jack Williams was one of Cheltenham's most successful competitors in motorcycle racing, but other forms of motorised two-wheeler sports also enjoyed a strong following. Motorcycle football attracted crowds of 10,000 or more at the Athletic Ground, bizarre though the sport seems today. Teams of six a side – including the goalie – raced round the pitch on motorbikes kicking a standard-sized football. They played thirty minutes each way to standard soccer rules, except that nobody bothered about off side. Nobody bothered to wear a crash helmet either, or any other protective clothing come to that, yet injuries were rare. If football on motorbikes strikes you as alarming, the notion of motorcycle and sidecar polo will be even more of a surprise. But the game was played, three a side and widely watched. So was motorbike surf boarding in which the competitor lay on a plank and was towed at speed behind a motorcycle. More conventionally, Cheltenham's A.R. Foster won the 1936 lightweight, Isle of Man TT race at a record average speed of 74.82mph – while on honeymoon.

The Cheltenham and County Cycling Club was founded in 1921 as a section of the Cheltenham and County Harriers. Still in the club's possession is the minutes book, which reveals 'The opening run was held on Sunday 23rd October 1921 and was to Broadway. Mr C. Brown, Hon Sec, photographed the members at Teddington Cross Hands, the starting point of most of the club races which followed.' Two years later 'at an Extraordinary General Meeting it was decided to discontinue the affiliation to the Harriers and form the club as a separate body to be called the Cheltenham and County Cycling Club'.

A mini golf course opened in Montpellier Gardens and women were admitted to the Cotswold Hills golf club.

*   *   *

Hosting the opening ceremony of coronation day was one of the last events staged at the Winter Garden, which had been a thorn in the town council's side for years past, as the *Chronicle* voiced: 'The future of the Winter Garden is a problem which has defied the council for 30 years'. Built in 1872, the great crystal palace occupied Imperial Gardens and was a wonder of Victorian engineering. It was also a white elephant – especially after the Town Hall was built in 1903. Concerts, roller skating, theatre, cinema, trade shows, conventions, formal dinners – all were tried inside the gigantic greenhouse, but none with sufficient success to pay the monumental maintenance cost of the place.

In the early '30s came a scheme to demolish the Winter Garden and put in its place a 'social rendezvous', with ice rink, swimming pool, restaurant, palm court, tennis courts . . . but the estimate of £130,000 made that idea a non-starter. Another plan was to convert the Winter Garden into a Kursaal, or continental-style health resort with spas, medical baths, water treatments, swimming, a gym . . . but once again the cost was prohibitive. Proposals galore came and went and all of them foundered on finance. In October 1938 the Winter Garden was declared dangerous and closed to the public.

*   *   *

August 1939 was a strange, surreal month when the world stood on the threshold of war. Cheltenham went about its business in the usual summertime way, but with constant reminders of imminent conflict. Blackout tests began on 4 July, becoming more frequent through August. But this didn't stop a capacity audience gathering at the Town Hall to see Joe Loss and his orchestra supported by the local band of Hector Davies and the Ambassadors.

A brace of anti-aircraft guns aroused much fascination when they arrived at St James's station to be towed through town to a newly installed battery at the racecourse. At the cricket festival crowds of 4,000 saw Gloucestershire – captained by Wally Hammond – beat the West Indies, Yorkshire and Middlesex.

Black and White coaches offered day trips to Weston for 7s 6d, or an evening jaunt to Birdlip for 1s 6d. In the Prom two 20,000-gallon water tanks appeared – one in front of Neptune's fountain, the other outside the general post office (now Hooper's) – to be used if the town centre was set ablaze by incendiary bombs. On top of Shirer and Lance's department store an air-raid siren was positioned.

Two George Formby films were showing in town in August 1939, and given that war was a matter of days away their titles were appropriate. *It's in the Air* was on at the Daffodil in Suffolk Parade, while the Gaumont in Winchcombe Street screened *Trouble's Brewing*.

Cheltenham was the wartime divisional control centre for Tewkesbury, Moreton-in-March, Northleach and the area in between. This meant that services such as civil defence, air raid precautions (ARP), ambulance, fire fighting, the provision of ration books and special police were organised from the town. The nerve centre of the ARP was Shirer and Lance's basement.

By the end of August 49,000 gas masks had been distributed to households in Cheltenham, but owing to an administrative error nobody in Whaddon received one. More masks were ordered, but Whaddon's residents went without until some time after war was declared on 3 September.

Gas mask drill for the children of St Paul's infant school.

Trench bomb shelters were dug in the grounds of all local schools. And at the boys grammar school, which then stood in the High Street, the central corridor was shored up with sturdy timbers to form a makeshift shelter. Shelters capable of accommodating 7,000 people in total were also constructed in the town centre. The largest – a trench with shored up sides, timber and corrugated iron roof, covered over with earth – was in Imperial Gardens. Others stood at the athletic ground, Royal Crescent and in the North Street car park of the Liberal Club. Smaller, brick-walled, concrete-roofed shelters were dotted about all over town.

September brought the first consignment of evacuees to Cheltenham. The mayor was at Lansdown station to welcome 267 schoolchildren from Birmingham, looking lost and unsure. Half a dozen double deckers drove the children to Naunton Park school, where they were billeted on homes in Leckhampton. Within a few days the influx of evacuees from the Midlands had increased Cheltenham's population by 2,000 and, not surprisingly, this caused tensions. An anonymous newcomer to the town wrote this rhyme, which appeared in the *Echo*:

> The town's so full of evacuees,
> Who do anything but please
> The inhabitants of Cheltenham.
> They're highbrow and aloof you see,
> And do not really care to be
> Anywhere near the evacuees
> Of educated Cheltenham.

Meeting in mid-September, the town magistrates imposed fines on those who'd infringed the blackout regulations. Miss Baylis, manager of the Majestic Hotel in Park Place, claimed she'd been unable to obtain enough material for the hotel's 200 windows, which was certainly true. All the town's stores had run out and declared that further supplies were not obtainable for the time being. Magistrates were told that the landlord of the Lamb Hotel in the High Street had made no effort to cover his windows, but instead had served customers in the dark, only turning on the lights at closing time to make sure they'd all gone. He was fined £3.

Hoods were placed over illuminated bollards. There were no street lights. Motorists were instructed to paint over their headlamps leaving only a small 2in window, covered with newspaper, for a little light to peep through. All advertising signs were switched off. The result was a dramatic increase in road accidents. Bus conductors also complained that the number of foreign coins being passed to them increased in the gloom.

Four thousand petrol ration books were issued in Cheltenham, each bearing the confusing message that possession of a ration book did not entitle the owner to petrol. Vehicles were classed as essential, semi-essential, or non-essential. And if yours was non-essential you locked it in the garage for the duration, unless you knew someone with access to coupons on the black market. Traders reverted to making deliveries by horse and cart, which resulted in a shortage of harnesses.

Cinemas and schools closed in the early weeks of the war and TV broadcasts were discontinued, not much of a hardship as almost nobody had a television. Coke, gas, electricity and coal were also on ration and reserve dumps of coal were set up by the local fuel controller, Mr G.G. Marshland, for use only in dire circumstances. Food rationing was introduced and soon queuing became a way of life.

Men and women queued to don the dark blue uniform of the ARP, and Auxiliary Fire Service. Other volunteer groups were formed to fill sand bags, dig trenches, build shelters and – in 1940 – remove iron railings to aid the war effort. Private houses with large cellars were opened by their owners as public air-raid shelters. Communal fruit preserving and jam making centres were established. There were eight in Cheltenham, where local people were taught how to make seasonal crops go further. There were bring and buys for the Hurricane Fund and Tank Week. Householders contributed their aluminium pots and pans to the Scrap for Spitfires campaign, and for the next six years fund raising became a way of life, along with pulling together and making do and mending.

The first evacuees to arrive in Cheltenham came from Birmingham.

Datelines

1920   Building began at the new council estate of St Marks on 27 April. The statue of William IV was moved from Imperial Square to Montpellier Gardens. The Cenotaph in memory of lives lost during the First World War was unveiled on 1 October by Major General Sir Robert Fanshawe.

1921   Cheltenham's first lady mayor, Ald. Clara F. Winterbotham, was elected. The new YMCA was opened in the Prom.

1922   The Lilleybrook Hotel (now Cheltenham Park Hotel) opened its doors to guests.

1923   The borough council built the bowling green in Ambrose Street, which was intended as a place of recreation for ex-servicemen.

1924   Governors of Cheltenham General Hospital reported a deficit of £2,200 and it was decided to adopt a system of payment by patients.

1925   Three tennis courts in Montpellier Gardens were replaced by a putting green.

1926   A £10,000 scheme to improve the River Chelt from College Road to Bath Road was approved by the town council. An earthquake was felt across the town on 25 August.

1927   Cheltenham composer Gustav Holst conducted his own work in the town hall.

1928   A sixteenth-century cottage in the Gloucester Road was taken down and reconstructed at Rossley Manor, Dowdeswell. A new school was opened at Andoversford.

1929   The Plough Hotel in Cheltenham's High Street was sold for £45,000. The town council paid £6,500 to buy Leckhampton Hill for the people of Cheltenham.

1930   Work began lifting tram lines to clear the way for motor buses. A thunderbolt was seen in the Promenade, when 'a large ball of fire shot across the sky with a trail of smoke'.

1931   The census showed Cheltenham's population to be 49,418.

1932   Plans for a new Winter Garden went on display. An 'all electric' demonstration house opened in Pittville Terrace.

1933   Protest rally by Cheltenham Unemployed Service Club. The Odeon cinema opened on the former site of the Congregational church in Winchcombe Street.

1934   The entry charge to Montpellier Gardens was dropped. The town's slum clearance programme razed poor quality housing in Grove Street, Exmouth Street, St Pauls, the Lower High Street area and elsewhere.

1935   Sandford Lido opened. St Gregory's convent closed. It became compulsory to have house numbers on residential houses. Newly built three-bedroomed semis in Mead Road at Leckhampton went on sale for £550.

1936   Miss Zanita Rulach of Kings Road, Cheltenham – the town's first woman pilot – was able to indulge her hobby at the newly opened Staverton Aerodrome, jointly owned by Cheltenham and Gloucester, which opened in July 1936. Royal Well bus station also opened.

1937   The Colonnade at the High Street end of the Prom was demolished and replaced by a new block of shops.

1938   The foundation stone of Pate's Grammar School for Girls was laid in Albert Road. Gas masks were distributed in town. The crematorium opened.

1939   The newly built Regal cinema opened in the Prom. There were 3,390 names in the Cheltenham telephone book. As war loomed air-raid shelters appeared around the town.

FIVE

Make Do and Mend 1940–59

From the moment war was declared almost everyone in the country was involved in one way or another. Men and women were called up to serve in the armed forces, work in factories, or contribute to the war effort. A genuine desire to 'do your bit' meant that those who were too young or too old to be conscripted eagerly joined a host of voluntary services. The result was a nation in uniform. ARP wardens, the Civil Defence Unit and First Aiders, most of whom had full-time day jobs, patrolled the streets at night. The Gloucestershire Special Police Constabulary under the command of Col Sir James Sleeman worked alongside the regular force. In the same way the Auxiliary Fire Service bolstered the sometimes stretched resources of their full-time counterparts.

The Women's Voluntary Service ran British Restaurants, which came to be called 'hot pots', where service personnel and others could obtain good, inexpensive food prepared from local produce.

When the Local Defence Volunteer force was formed early in the war, resources were so limited that arm bands were the only items of uniform available to its members. This was remedied later when the LDV was renamed the Home Guard. Workplaces such as Smiths Industries in Bishops Cleeve and Webb's brickworks in Cheltenham had their own platoons.

Voluntary organisations such as the Salvation Army, Church Army and YMCA ran mobile canteens. The YMCA's was run by Mrs Bagnall and her daughter Joy, who dispensed tea, sandwiches and smiles from an Austin Seven van. Among many other tasks they met and helped to arrange accommodation for children evacuated from the Midlands who arrived locally. The YMCA also provided static canteens for service people in transit, such as the ones at Cheltenham's Lansdown railway station and behind the Municipal Offices in Royal Well. These were well used by GIs, who flooded

Above: Land Army women at work in Boddington.
Below: Auxiliary Fire Service volunteers in the Promenade.

Dowty Home Guard at Arle Court.

the town when Cheltenham became the HQ for the American Forces of Supply in the build up to D-Day.

*　　*　　*

Anti-aircraft guns appeared around the town. At the end of Sandy Pluck Lane, Bentham, was a four gun anti-aircraft gun station. Another stood at Hayden Farm. This was manned, among others, by 495 (M) HAA Battery B Company. This posting had the advantage of being near the House in the Tree pub, kept during the war years by Mr and Mrs Drew. The anti-aircraft emplacement at Prestbury Park boasted a pair of 3.7in guns. At the beginning of the war the 1st Glos Hussars were stationed at Prestbury Park. There was plenty of room for tank training at the racecourse, but accommodation was sparse, so most of the men made themselves comfortable in the stables. Despite the war, racing took place and as the date of the next meeting drew close, the Hussars were told they'd have to move themselves and their tanks out. The men were ordered to vacate the stables, making sure they left them spick and span, so that the horses could move in.

*　　*　　*

Schoolchildren were involved in the war effort. At the new Pate's Grammar School for Girls in Albert Road local pupils attended in the morning, while evacuees from King

Edward's High School, Birmingham, moved in for the afternoon. The boys of Cheltenham Grammar shared with Moseley Grammar (also from Birmingham) and corridors of the High Street school were shored up with heavy timbers in an effort to limit possible blast damage. Pupils were divided into squads and led by teachers for night-time duties, such as ARP work and firewatching. Boys from the school also constructed Morrison shelters in local homes.

Pupils from local schools were released at harvest time to help farmers with haymaking and potato picking. In addition, many schools turned over their playing fields to agriculture. In villages it was more usual for local pupils and evacuees to share the same school day. Leckhampton C of E Primary accommodated twenty-two evacuees alongside its local intake. ARP trenches dug in the school grounds were used on a number of occasions. On 25 July 1940 German planes were spotted in the area and as surrounding anti-aircraft guns boomed into action schoolchildren filed into the slit trenches. During holidays the school remained open to serve milk and meals to needy evacuees, some of them living in the nearby parish hall without cooking facilities.

*   *   *

Boys from the Grammar School put up Morrison bomb shelters in homes around the town.

Scrap for Spitfires. Metal items were taken to collection points around the town by locals. This one was in Francis Street.

The first German bomb to fall on British soil in the Second World War landed at Hoy in the Orkneys on 17 October 1939. Gloucestershire escaped the Luftwaffe's attentions until 18 June 1940, when the Bristol Aircraft Company at Filton was hit. Cheltenham's first air raid alert came eight days later, although bombs intended for the town had previously fallen at Nether Westcote near Bourton-on-the-Water. During the second half of 1940 the frequency and intensity of attacks increased. On 25 August a device fell at Hesters Way, but failed to explode. A few days later two oil bombs narrowly missed a searchlight position at Prestbury.

In August 1940 the Luftwaffe launched its first massed attack on a British city. Liverpool was the target and 150 bombers were involved, but it seems likely that some of them lost their way. Bombs were strewn across Brockworth's GAC site, but little damage was sustained. At Staverton, however, three airmen were killed when a bomb fell on a barrage balloon post.

In mid-October three railway personnel were injured in Cheltenham when high explosives fell on the LMSR goods yard between Arle Road and Tewkesbury Road. Then on the 16th of that month a lone German raider strafed the streets of

Clearing bomb damage in Stoneville Street.

Brockworth, causing damage to houses that had to be evacuated. The plane then flew on to Churchdown and machine gunned Hurran's nurseries, perhaps mistaking the glasshouses for aeroplane hangars. Five days later a single Junkers 88 attacked GAC during the works' lunchtime. Three high explosive bombs were dropped, landing harmlessly on open ground. An oil bomb, however, fell on to the roof of number 7 machine shop. Damage to the building was not extensive, but a number of employees were killed and others injured.

One of the most devastating raids of the war, named *Mondlicht Sonate* by Hermann Goering, razed much of Coventry in mid-November, killing 500 and injuring 800 more. There were eighty-one other raids on provincial towns that same moonlit night, including two bombs that fell at Dowdeswell and three near Northleach. Four days later Cheltenham was the target, when eighteen delayed action bombs rained on the town. One smashed through the roof of a house in Pilley Crescent, Leckhampton, and became embedded in the kitchen floor without going off. Other bombs landed at Southfield Farm in nearby Church Road, in Burrows playing field and the allotments in Hall Road, adjacent to Leckhampton Primary School. The railway bridge in Shurdington Road was narrowly missed.

The destruction reached its crescendo on Wednesday 11 December 1940. At 7.20 p.m. siting flares were dropped over Cheltenham and ten minutes later incendiary, high explosive and oil bombs fell – over 100 in total. H.H. Martyn's Sunningend Works were hit and set ablaze, which served to direct other Luftwaffe raiders to the scene. Half of Stoneville Street was demolished when a large bomb landed on the railway embankment nearby. Ten were killed, some of them children. On the other side of Gloucester Road a gas holder was hit, as was Parkwood Mansion flats in Shurdington Road where five died. Someone who must have thought himself the luckiest man alive that night was Cyril Price, who incidentally played cricket for Cheltenham. Cyril was watching the dramatic events from Pilley railway bridge in Old Bath Road, when a bomb fell on it. The device passed clean through and exploded on the line below, destroying the bridge and leaving Cyril tottering on the edge of a gaping chasm, but unharmed. As a temporary measure a wooden footway for pedestrians was strung over the hole where Pilley bridge had been. Crossing it was referred to by locals as 'walking the plank'. Pilley had the distinction of being the last war-damaged bridge in the country to be repaired. A long argument raged about who was responsible for meeting

Stoneville Street. Six hundred were made homeless following the raids of 11 December 1940.

the cost of reconstruction – the town council, British Railways or the Ministry of Transport. The matter was even raised in the House of Commons before the Old Bath Road bridge finally re-opened in 1954.

Other bombs on that fateful night in 1940 fell on fine houses in Parabola Road, Christchurch Road and Lansdown Road and on more modest residences in Merrivale Gardens and St Marks. The fronts of four houses collapsed in Kipling Road when a bomb fell between Shelley Road and Spencer Road leaving a large crater. Cheltenham police headquarters in the town centre (now the Countryside Agency) suffered damage and the Black and White coach station's main building was flattened. So violent was the latter explosion that a single decker coach was lifted bodily over the perimeter wall, killing a passer by.

In the aftermath of the 11 December 1940 raid 600 townspeople were made homeless and had to find temporary accommodation in local schools and parish halls. Mains water was cut off and rail links severed. But by first light, when gangs of volunteers and service people set to the formidable task of clearing up, Union Jacks fluttered defiantly from the debris.

*   *   *

It wasn't only the Luftwaffe that was wreaking destruction on Cheltenham. The town council also got in on the act by using the war as an excuse to rid itself of that long-time burden the Winter Garden. A morsel of this magnificent monolith can be glimpsed to this day behind the open-air bar in Imperial Gardens. Between the beer taps and the Town Hall is a short passageway, where you'll notice that the cream and red chequerwork bricks to your right don't match the Town Hall's stone facing. Those bricks are all that remain of what was one of the most remarkable buildings ever to grace the town – Cheltenham Winter Garden.

From the ivy-clad, brickwork base, liberally adorned with flying buttresses, soared a great glasshouse roof supported on arching, cast-iron spans. Campanile-like towers stood at each corner and the central atrium lofted airily to a height of 100ft. This was indeed a celebration of Victorian architectural engineering at its most audacious. Inside the decor displayed eclectic influences: part palm court, part Turkish sultan's boudoir, a sprinkling of 'Egypt – land of the pharaohs', plus motifs from the Indian sub-continent. The Winter Garden made a bold, imperial statement. But commercially the place was destined to be a dead loss.

Cheltenham's own crystal palace was constructed in 1879 to a design by J.T. Darby. Its intended purpose, so we learn from a report of the time, was to provide 'A large concert room and other accessories, calculated to afford recreation and amusement to the upper classes'. In no time at all it became as clear as the roof that the upper classes had no wish to recreate there and were not amused. The building was capable of

War provided the excuse to demolish the Winter Garden.

accommodating huge hordes of people, but was largely unsuitable for anything much. In October 1893, by way of example, the Winter Garden provided the venue for the third Cheltenham Triennial Music Festival. An impressive pipe organ was installed and over 500 performers took part on a stage ample enough to seat a complete chorus, full orchestra, soloists and the conductor on his podium with room to spare. But the Winter Garden had all the acoustic virtues of an aircraft hangar and if it rained during a concert the thrumming on the glass roof did battle with the performers.

Various proprietors took control of the crouching colossus, couldn't make it pay and moved on. Then in 1895 the town council bought the building, primarily because nobody else would. What to do with the Winter Garden caused much scratching of municipal heads. In the search to find a function the auditorium was tried as an exhibition hall. Trade shows were staged there. Auctions were held in a bid to help cover the overheads. The occasional travelling circus moved in. In the early years of the twentieth century the huge hall was thrown open to roller skaters. Then it was a cinema (or 'Kinema' as the makeshift sign outside read). But any hope of succeeding as a venue for entertainment disappeared when the Town Hall appeared in 1904, and right next door come to that. Time was plainly running out for this expensive, mammoth-sized

The interior of the Winter Garden.

example of a white elephant. By the time war came in 1939 the wonderful and hopeless Winter Garden was an ailing albatross around the council's neck. Repairs had been neglected for years. The building's safety was questionable. And worst of all the place served no purpose. On the fabricated excuse that the structure provided the Luftwaffe with a landmark, the decision to demolish was taken in September 1940. The council breathed a quiet sigh of relief as the men with hammers arrived.

*   *   *

Staverton airport was a cosmopolitan place to be during the war. As home to No. 31 Elementary and Reserve Flying School, plus No. 6 Air Observer Navigation School, which moved to Staverton from Shoreham in Sussex, airmen from Britain, Canada,

Australia, New Zealand, Poland, France, Belgium and other allied countries all rubbed shoulders. De Havilland Rapide, Tiger Moth and Avro Anson aircraft were the most commonly used trainers. But in addition to flying, personnel attended six-week theory courses, sixty at a time, before moving to RAF stations for the final stages of training. Sometimes accommodation for trainees couldn't be found locally and they had to make do with tents pitched along Bamfurlong Lane.

Later in the war No. 2 Elementary Flying School relocated to Staverton from Bristol, as barrage balloons around the Bristol Aircraft Company site were a hazard. In the latter years of the war Sir Alan Cobham's company Flight Refuelling Ltd moved to Staverton. One of its experiments involved towing Hurricanes behind Wellington bombers so as to extend the fighters' range and enable them to provide support on long distance missions. The idea didn't work too well, as the slipstream from the Wellington made controlling the Hurricane in its wake extremely difficult.

Lancasters flew into Staverton from time to time, which was no mean feat for the pilots involved, as the heavy four-engined bombers required a longer runway than the local aerodrome could provide. One Lanc overshot and ended up straddling Bamfurlong Lane, while another came down in a field on the edge of Staverton village. Incidentally, next time you're passing along Bamfurlong Lane and draw level with the main runway, take a look at what seems to be a sunken pile of bricks covered in ivy and undergrowth. It is, in fact, a well-preserved pill box built in 1940. There used to be another one protecting the Churchdown end of the airport, but it was demolished in the 1950s when the runway was extended.

Staverton was home to the Rotol Flight Test Dept, Folland Aircraft Ltd, GAC Flight Test Dept and other organisations that tested aeronautical developments during the war. With so much experimental work and so many trainee flyers centred on the airport, it's hardly surprising that accidents and incidents happened frequently. One wartime story recalls that a young pilot crashed his Tiger Moth to the rear of the Plough Inn on the old A40 Cheltenham road. Struggling from the wreckage, he staggered into the pub to order a stiff drink and was told by the landlord he'd have to wait his turn to be served, just like all the other crashed pilots who used the bar.

*   *   *

War converted the town into a cosmopolitan place and the uniforms of pretty well all forces on the Allied side were seen at the Cheltenham Services Club in Regent Street. Its purpose was to provide a venue that would contribute 'to the moral welfare of Cheltenham, as well as to the pleasure and well being of the forces'. To ensure that the club's activities were suitably decorous, a governing council was formed comprising representatives from the forces, Cheltenham corporation, the Church, Women's Voluntary Service and the YMCA. The club, which was run entirely by volunteers, was opened on 5 November 1943 by Sir Archibald Sinclair, Secretary of State for the Air. It boasted a spacious main hall with a stage that was used by local amateur dramatic and services groups, and bands. At one of the first evening entertainments the Gloucester National Service Club's orchestra played a programme of light music, well enough for them to be invited back. There were easy chairs and sofas, table tennis, darts, cards, chess, draughts and discussion groups on Wednesdays with speakers provided by the Army Education Office, and a kitchen serving light refreshments, homemade buns, cakes and sandwiches. Membership was open to women and men serving in the British and Allied forces and cost 1s per year. Within three months of opening the club had 3,000 members – Brits, Poles, Latvians, Lithuanians, Norwegians, New Zealanders, Australians. . . . And when Uncle Sam turned Cheltenham into a supply centre, GIs by the train, truck and Jeep load introduced jazz and razzmatazz to the Club's usual fare of table tennis and iced buns.

*   *   *

In the build up to the D-Day invasion of Nazi Europe, the American forces almost took Cheltenham over. They occupied numerous buildings including Pittville Pump Room. The Queen's Hotel became a US officers' club and they erected nissen huts in town parks. After years of only occasional use Cheltenham synagogue was suddenly filled to overflowing when Jewish servicemen arrived in town along with thousands of GIs from Uncle Sam's Forces of Supply. A plaque presented by those servicemen in gratitude for the hospitality and welcome they received from the congregation can be seen in Cheltenham synagogue today.

The rural peace that usually resided in the parish of Cowley with Coberley was ousted when hordes of construction workers and military personnel arrived from the US to build themselves a hospital at Ullenwood. Heavy Chevrolet trucks rumbled along the previously peaceful country lanes bringing tons of building materials and equipment, all shipped in from America. To local people, who by 1943 were well used to mending and making do, the transatlantic new arrivals were exotic indeed. They had so much of everything. The 110th US General Hospital became operational in July 1944. Some of the huts can be seen to this day if you walk along Greenway Lane, which skirts the site. In some cases the single-storey, brick buildings have been converted for light industrial use and double-glazed window units are now manufactured where US servicemen once had their wounds tended. Other huts just stand empty, a silent reminder of distant days. When it opened Ullenwood was a self-contained medical complex providing beds for 1,000 patients, but before long the hospital was able to accommodate twice that number. Wounded American soldiers, sailors and airmen arrived in Cheltenham by train at Leckhampton station and were then ferried up the hill to Ullenwood by ambulance, or truck. In those days the US

The post-Second World War Prom looked much the same, but elsewhere Cheltenham was on the threshold of change.

army had a policy of racial segregation, so black and white service people were treated in separate wards.

American casualties increased as the Allied armies moved eastwards through Europe after the Normandy landings, which meant that at times Ullenwood didn't have enough beds. On these occasions temporary wards were set up in tents pitched between the rows of huts, and it was the black soldiers who had to endure being under canvas. Imagine what that must have been like in the bitter winter of 1944 when snow lay on the ground for some weeks.

The commanding officer of the camp was Lt-Col John L. Berry, who sent this message to all the patients the Christmas after Ullenwood opened: 'To the brave wounded and sick patients, I extend my heartfelt sympathy and hope that you will soon be well and strong again. I admire you for the undaunted courage and complacency manifested by your cheerful smiles, your patient tolerance of unalterable conditions, and your willingness to help others in a more serious plight.' Lt-Col Berry returned to visit Ullenwood in the early 1960s, by which time the camp stood empty.

Besides its medical wards, the hospital accommodated nurses, doctors and other staff in barracks. There was an orthodontic department, a mess hall, NCO club and the camp had its own post office. Along with operating theatres, there was a film theatre where the latest Hollywood productions were shown.

Convalescing soldiers sometimes amused themselves by painting on the hut walls and their subjects – the skyscrapers of New York, farms of the mid-west plains, oil wells of Texas – were no doubt inspired by homesickness. Remnants of these artistic outpourings can be seen at Ullenwood to this day. Patients who were mobile and those who looked after them became regulars at the Air Balloon pub, a half-mile stroll away, where they were introduced to the British tradition of drinking warm beer (though not very much, as it was on ration). The alternative tipple (and not on ration) was that Gloucestershire speciality – cider. A gent who still lives in Shurdington struck up a useful arrangement with the Americans during the war. He arranged to collect the camp leftovers to feed to his pigs, which brought him into contact with many GIs, wounded and recuperating, to whom he introduced the delights of scrumpy and perry. Before long a mutually beneficial black-market trade developed. In return for regular supplies of locally made booze, the enterprising villager collected 'pigswill' that included cheeses, hams, chocolate and other goodies that were unobtainable in wartime Britain.

Ullenwood officially stood down from wartime service in September 1945, though the camp then immediately assumed a new role. As the Americans moved out the Polish Army moved in, and for the next couple of years the camp became Ullenwood Basic Unit 501 (training and regrouping). Following this, Ullenwood became a civil defence centre. Then in the early 1970s, when the dictator Idi Amin expelled tens of thousands of Asians from Uganda, Ullenwood was prepared as a reception camp, though it was never used for this purpose. Within the grounds of the site is a large underground bunker, which was constructed as one of a dozen seats of local government in Britain set aside for use in the event of nuclear war. The top-secret bunker (which just about everyone in the county knew was there) was owned by the Home Office until 1985, when it was passed on to the county council. Then, with the end of the cold war, plans were mooted to turn the subterranean stronghold into a store for the county archive, but that didn't happen either.

Whatever the future for Ullenwood may be (at the time of writing it is up for sale), it certainly had a colourful past. Those empty huts you'll see if you take a stroll along Greenway Lane recall a time when part of the parish of Cowley with Coberley was as American as apple pie.

*   *   *

The war against Nazi Germany ended on 8 May 1945 with a heady mixture of elation and relief. There were dancing and street parties. Schools staged fancy-dress celebrations and, despite acute shortages, communities managed to beg, borrow, or steal enough food to feast. But the joy was short lived. With Britain bankrupt, the end of the war presaged a long decade of austerity. Rationing continued. Queuing remained a fact of life. Ahead lay a lot more mending and making do.

*   *   *

Cheltenham in the '50s was changing fast. The population stood at about 60,000 and was rising apace because of the good employment prospects presented by Dowty's, the recent arrival of GCHQ and the expansion of engineering firms such as Walker Crossweller at Whaddon and Smiths Industries in Bishops Cleeve. Another local employer was Cheltenham Caravans. The company exhibited at the 1952 Earl's Court motor show, when four of its models were on display, the Eland, Antelope, Gazelle and Bison. The latter was newly launched and received an enthusiastic review from *The Autocar* in its London Show

Dowty's Arle Court complex with wartime camouflage on the factory roof.

Work on Princess Elizabeth Way began in 1951.

issue: 'Cheltenham's new model is the Bison, a 15'4" van with ex-works weight of 17 cwt. It is typical of Cheltenham ovoid styling. The interior is in limed oak and, as will be seen by the Show visitor, has a very attractive layout. It is unusual to see a van of this size with a single panelled roof.' The report went on to reveal that plastic crockery 'bearing the Cheltenham mark of three concentric "C"s and made of a new material which does not taste or become rough with use is to be a standard feature of all Cheltenham models'.

With so many people arriving in the town, local removal companies, such as Pickfords in Granley Road and Elliot Brothers, with depots in Princes Street and Bouncers Lane, Prestbury, were kept busy. To house the incomers, estates were developed at Hesters Way and Benhall, gobbling up what had previously been open fields and humpty-dumps. Coronation Square and Princess Elizabeth Way are names that hint heavily at the time when Cheltenham's largest housing estate was built. Started in the early 1950s, some 3,000 new homes appeared at Hesters Way by the end of the decade, a continuation of the council's housing programme, which had been interrupted by the war.

Work on Princess Elizabeth Way began in 1951. This swathe of tarmac joining the Tewkesbury and Gloucester Roads was the spine of the new estate. Scott House,

PARISH OF ST. MARK'S
CHELTENHAM

Order of Service

for the

Laying of the

Foundation-Stone

of

St. Aidan's Church

in the

Parish of St. Mark's, Cheltenham

by

The Lord Bishop of Gloucester

(The Right Rev. W. M. ASKWITH, D.D.)

Thursday, April 9th 1959

at 4 p.m.

SHENTONS PRINTING WORKS, CHELTENHAM

Wilson House and other purpose-built flats lined the route to its dog-leg at Coronation Square, then the broad thoroughfare continued towards the A40. At this junction was the enclave of single-storey buildings that in wartime had been occupied by the American Forces of Supply, but in 1952 became GCHQ when the organisation transferred to Cheltenham from Bletchley Park. This relocation swelled the town's population and the flats at the lower end of Princess Elizabeth Way were built to accommodate employees at the government agency.

The foundation stone of another estate landmark, St Aidan's church, was laid on 9 April 1959 by the Bishop of Gloucester, the Right Revd Wilfred Askwith. He was attended by G.R. Woodhams, the vicar of St Mark's, three parish curates, the Revds Messrs Wilkinson, Betts and Whitehead, and the parish lady worker Sister McKemey. A large congregation gathered for the open-air service, wading through the building site mud to stand in the rain and sing hymns. Copies of the parish magazine and Monkscroft school magazine were set into the mortar beneath the foundation stone. While the new church was rising on its concrete ribs, Hesters Way worshippers met at the first St Aidan's church. Affectionately known as 'the hut' and erected in 1955, this single-storey prefabrication stood behind the present building. (By the way, Cheltenham in Pennsylvania, USA – a town founded by Tobias Leech and Richard Wall who emigrated to the new world from Arle – also has a St Aidan's church, named after the early British saint.) Further down Princess Elizabeth Way is St Thomas More's.

New houses, like these in Church Road, Leckhampton, sprang up on the outskirts of town.

Built after St Aidan's, this was Cheltenham's second Roman Catholic church, hexagonal in shape and at the time considered daringly modern in design.

Monkscroft Junior School opened in 1954 with Miss Chandler as the first head. Its namesake senior school (now the site of Gloscat) came a few years later with Mr Tiplady as head.

Until Hesters Way was raised, Shakespeare Road ended in a wire fence beyond which lay the humpty-dumps. Another local name for the land on which both Monkscroft schools, Goldsmith Road and Coronation Square were built was the aeroplane field. Exactly why the patch was so named isn't altogether clear. It may be because in the pioneering days of aviation an air day was held on the site, probably by a local flier named B.C. Huckes, when dare-devils could, for a few shillings, endure an open cockpit flight over the town. Another possible explanation is Hubert Philpotts. He was chauffeur to the Unwin family of Arle Court, now Cheltenham Film Studios. In 1910 Philpotts flew a monoplane he had taken two years to make himself. This had a frame of American spruce and bamboo with a propeller of laminated mahogany, a wing span of 26ft and an Italian, three-cylinder Anzani engine. The amateur aviator kept his homemade machine at Arle Court, so his take-offs and landings were likely to have

Interior design, 1950s.

Following years of austerity the town centre was decidedly dowdy and demolition, rather than renovation, was the preferred option. AA Motors' premises and much more of North Street were razed.

been on what became known as the aeroplane field. There is another possibility. On 4 September 1940 a De Havilland Tiger Moth made an emergency landing at Hesters Way. The pilot, L.A.C. Williams, was injured but survived.

While new housing estates were under construction on the outskirts, large areas of the town centre were being demolished. Doris's café disappeared along with one side of Pittville Street, and Albion Street was widened. This involved the removal of Barnes's newsagents, Jackson's the pork butcher (both neighbours of the Odeon) and other well-known shops. The North Place car showrooms of AA Motors were demolished, ironically, to ease traffic congestion. In the mid-1950s Royal Well bus station was developed with its line of prefabricated shelters. The Gas Company office on the corner of North Street and Albion Street was one of the town's grandest structures, a resounding statement of high Victorian architecture. By the end of the '50s this elegant edifice had been reduced to hard core and the gas company had set up shop in newly built, lino-floored, Pittville Street premises, complete with vinyl furnishings.

*   *   *

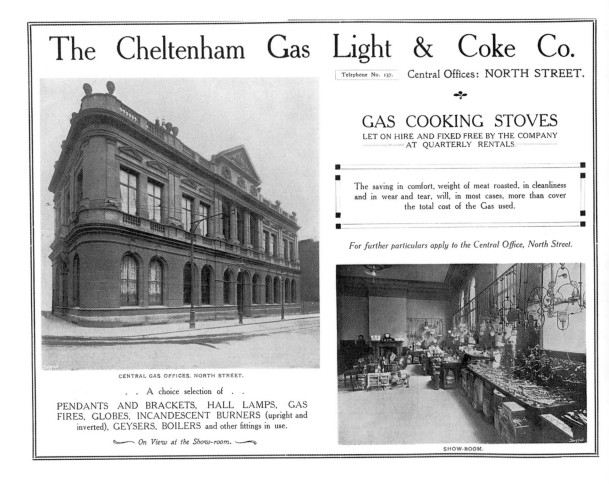

The Cheltenham Gas Light & Coke Co.

Telephone No. 137.   Central Offices: NORTH STREET.

GAS COOKING STOVES

LET ON HIRE AND FIXED FREE BY THE COMPANY
AT QUARTERLY RENTALS.

The saving in comfort, weight of meat roasted, in cleanliness
and in wear and tear, will, in most cases, more than cover
the total cost of the Gas used.

For further particulars apply to the Central Office, North Street.

CENTRAL GAS OFFICES, NORTH STREET.

. . A choice selection of . .

PENDANTS AND BRACKETS, HALL LAMPS, GAS
FIRES, GLOBES, INCANDESCENT BURNERS (upright and
inverted), GEYSERS, BOILERS and other fittings in use.

On View at the Show-room.

SHOW-ROOM.

Novel though the notion seems today, in the 1950s you could buy groceries, fruit, vegetables, fish and meat at numerous shops in the town centre. Wet fish was wonderfully displayed in all its icy slipperiness on the slabs of Olives, MacFisheries and Iddles in the High Street. Peter Robinson (where W.H. Smith now stands) was a mecca for ladies with an eye for fashion, while jewellers Saqui & Laurence at the junction of High Street and Pittville Street provided the accompanying baubles. Marguerite's, the florist, stood on the corner of Crescent Terrace and Clarence Parade, and for a portrait of someone special you probably chose Raeburn Photographic near Pittville Gates. It was almost a rite of passage for Cheltenham children to be snapped in their Sunday best at Raeburn's studio, which – it's sad but true to report – was lacking in the props department. Little girls were always pictured with the same cuddly horse, boys with the same tin model car.

Banks was a well-established stationer and bookshop in the Prom, and by the 1950s its nearby retail neighbours included Nixon's china and glassware, the patisserie and confiserie of Maison Kunz, Ayris – a well-known frock shop, Arthur Jack's the jewellers,

Beetham and Clark chemist, F.J. Foice's hairdressing salon and Dale Forty, selling musical instruments, records, sheet music and wireless sets.

James Dicks & Sons occupied the town centre side of the High Street/St George's Street junction. The business was something of a local institution, having been on the site since the firm was founded in 1871, originally as a drapers. Over the ensuing years the business expanded into other nearby properties. China and carpet departments were opened on the opposite corner of St George's Street, a location that later became Foster Brothers menswear. (Many a local pupil began their school career in a blazer from Fosters.) Dicks Corner was home to another local landmark, the Pepper Pot. This public loo was shaped like the condiment container after which it was colloquially known and stood, inconveniently, in the middle of the busy junction on a traffic roundabout. Loo and roundabout were demolished in 1957.

During the '50s and '60s the shop on the out-of-town corner of Ambrose Street and the High Street was Charles Dickens, a tobacconist. The firm had another branch in the promontory premises opposite Littlewoods that's now a cobbler's shop.

In 1951, by the way, you could have stayed at the Moorend Park Hotel for a week, full board, for 7 guineas, while you'd have paid £8 1s a week at the Fleece, which stood on the corner of the High Street and Henrietta Street (originally called Fleece Lane).

*   *   *

1955 was a golden threshold for live, popular entertainment in Cheltenham. In that year Winchcombe Street's Odeon began staging acts; for most local people it was their first opportunity to see in the flesh stars they'd heard on the wireless, or (less likely) seen on TV. When Billy 'Wakey-Wakey!' Cotton and his Band took to the cinema's stage they were already a national institution. The band's hugely popular Sunday lunchtime radio show (preceded by 'Two-Way Family Favourites' and followed by Jimmy Clithero in 'The Clithero Kid') was as much a part of most people's lives as roast beef and Yorkshire pud. Harry Secombe, Peter Sellers, Michael Bentine and Spike Milligan – collectively known as The Goons – brought their anarchic humour to Cheltenham, and cult followers in the audience cheered as Grytpype-Thynne, Col Bloodnok, Little Jim and Eccles came to life. Max Wall provided more off-beat humour with his funny walks, lugubrious delivery and never quite playing the piano. Smooth trumpeter Eddie Calvert rounded off the 1955 season of live entertainment at the Odeon. Jimmy Young's six-night residence in May 1956 must have been like a home-coming for the Forest of Dean-born singing star. Tickets were 2s 6d to 5s.

In 1957 Petula Clark came to town, supported by comedian Ken Dodd. But the sensation of the year was Bill Haley, who arrived with his Comets on 9 March to play a one-night stand. Quaint though it seems today, the kiss curled, glitter jacketed Mr Haley and his portly, almost middle-aged Comets were widely considered a threat to public order. Their 'Rock Around the Clock' hit of 1955 had (according to establishment sources) incited violence and was the devil's music incarnate. Would the Odeon still be standing after Mr Haley & Co.'s show? Would all the seats be slashed? Such were the fears voiced in Cheltenham, but needless to say the answers to those questions proved to be 'Yes' and 'No'. A few local teddy boys – drape jackets, quiffed hair, crepe-soled shoes – danced in the aisles with their teddy girls – full skirts, petticoats galore, bobby sox – but not a flick-knife flashed.

Not until the late 1950s did television make much of an impact. Sets were startlingly expensive, programmes were only broadcast for a few hours a day and much of the viewing output comprised interludes such as the potter's wheel or the watermill. For most people, the wireless was the thing. During the decade variety shows from the BBC Midlands studios in Birmingham often included acts from Gloucestershire. Forest of Dean comedian Chick Fowler performed monologues in a rich rural brogue. Gaffer and Gavotte was another comedy act from the locality, and shows were sometimes compered by Tom Hay, who when not cracking gags on the radio was a postman.

Vincent Ladbrook's Band, which played at Cheltenham Motor Club dances in the Town Hall for many years, became popular on the wireless, as did the Hector Davies Band, Billy Derek's Orchestra and the Astoria Dance Band. Many local toes no doubt tapped to the sound of Trevor Brookes's Band, the Harry Etheridge Band and – something of an acquired taste perhaps – the Billy Thomas Accordion Band. Just occasionally the overnight celebrity of being on the BBC went to the performers' heads. The locally based Al Durrant Six played but once over the airwaves before its reincarnation as The Al Durrant Broadcast Six.

Teenagers, of course, were invented in the 1950s. If you were one of them you may have bounced gently up and down on the Town Hall's sprung dance floor to local musical maestros such as the Bill Hartland Band with vocalist Benny Aspey, the Al Kessel Band, or the Tilley Brothers Band (formed by twins Peter and Paul).

No whistle-stop tour of the local entertainment scene in the 1950s would be complete without mention of the extraordinary Vladimir Lavinski. For a few months in 1952 he hit the national headlines when he declared that he was the reincarnation of Franz Liszt. His name was actually David Seccombe and he was born in Malta on 22 February 1930, the son of a naval commander. Just before the Second World War the family moved to Tewkesbury where they bought the Shuthonger Manor Hotel. Music was in the blood and David, who attended Uppingham School, had a grandmother who was an accomplished pianist. David showed promise on the instrument too. At the age of twenty-one he moved to Cheltenham and took up residence in the Royston Hotel. It was now that his eccentricities began to blossom. Dressed in knee length boots, a swirling cape about his shoulders and a bloom on either lapel, David Seccombe waved his swagger stick and became Vladimir Lavinski. According to people who remember him, David, or Vlad, was a well-spoken, intellectual type – but fanciful. He fancied, for example, that he was 'One of the world's great pianists' and billed himself as such when playing at balls in the town hall.

The national papers heard of Cheltenham's sartorially exotic ivory tickler and gave him a great deal of exposure. 'Music is my life,' he told the *Daily Mail*, 'but I like golf too.' He was likened to Percy Grainger, but more for his fanciful foibles than his musical ability. Flushed with celebrity, Vladimir Lavinski arranged a tour of performances with dates set for Croydon, Bournemouth and even the Wigmore Hall, London. At the latter prestigious venue, where he was billed as 'The Paginini of the Piano', Vlad's entrance was greeted with bemusement by an audience not knowing if it was about to witness genius, or farce. Placing a framed portrait of Liszt on the piano and clutching a cigar between his teeth, Vladimir launched into Beethoven's Sonata in C minor – the 'Moonlight'. According to reviews of the time it started off well enough. Then Vlad left bits out. And added some passages of his own. The audience laughed, left . . . and that was the end of his career as a professional pianist.

*   *   *

Cars mothballed during the Second World War took to the roads again, especially when petrol became more freely available after rationing finished and branded fuel was

Rodney Road. Cars that had not been used during the war were brought out of hibernation when hostilities ended.

reintroduced in 1953. Despite this, horse-drawn vehicles were still a familiar sight about town. Coal from the Co-op was delivered in this way and the rag-and-bone man with his piebald pony and incomprehensible street-cry was a local character. Milk arrived by horse and cart too, although the Gloucestershire Dairy's fleet of red and white electric floats, operating from the depot in Prestbury Road or buzzing about the dairy in Imperial Lane, showed the way forward.

Parking was a growing problem and in 1953 the mayor, T.L. Thompson, thought he had the answer. On a civic visit to Cheltenham, Pennsylvania, His Worship had seen parking meters, a novelty yet to reach these shores at the time. At a meeting of the town council the motion was forwarded that Cheltenham should become the first town in Britain to introduce parking meters. 'No, please, no!' came the response from one councillor. 'It isn't British! by which I mean it isn't cricket! Let parking meters stay in America!' The council voted against meters and Cheltenham's parking problem survived intact.

By the early 1950s business at the Black & White coach station was once again brisk. The company invested in a replacement fleet of thirty flat-fronted Leyland Royal Tigers. No doubt many former passengers now of gently ripening years have vivid memories of travelling, or being stuck in traffic jams, aboard one of these stylish thirty-three seaters. In those pre-motorway days the trip to London was a major expedition and one undertaken in stages. First stop out from Cheltenham along the meandering A40 was Northleach, then Burford and Witney, and at Oxford everyone got off to stretch their legs, eat packed lunches and slurp from a Thermos. Thus refreshed it was back on the bus, and next stop High Wycombe. Excitement mounted at the Uxbridge stop, because London really was just up the road now. But between Uxbridge and the final destination of Victoria came the inevitable congestion of Western Avenue and the slow crawl past the Hoover building.

*   *   *

Café culture found its feet once more after the shortages imposed by wartime. The Cadena had two branches, one in the Prom where Habitat is now and another near Lloyd's Bank in the High Street. A special three-course lunch at The Cake Basket in Montpellier Walk was priced at half a crown in the mid-1950s and 'Dainty' teas were advertised and served from 3 until 5 p.m. Brunners in Winchcombe Street sold cakes from a ground-floor shop, or you could chomp these baked-on-the-premises confections in the first-floor café. Another family-run concern was Maison Kunz, legendary locally for the acute yumminess of its chocolate fancies, though perhaps lacking the wider appeal of Geraldine's. If you can't recall Geraldine's and are wondering where this fine eating house was once located, face the Municipal Offices, run your eye along to the right and when you reach the building at the end of the terrace – now a pub – you've got it.

The Milk Bar, which stood in the Colonnade, heralded a new age. Very '50s in style, it boasted a feast of Formica and chrome which met the eye, while the gurgle of the Gagglia met the ear. Frothy coffee in glass cups was sipped from tubular steel stool perches as the young customers eyed themselves and each other in etched mirrors galore. This was Cheltenham's own coffee bar, just like the one cinema goers saw in the new Cliff Richard film *Expresso Bongo*. In most Cheltenham cafés the swish of pearl on twin set predominated. But in the Milk Bar the rustle of pac-a-macs was punctuated by the nearby popping of Vespas. Like much else in the town, café society was changing.

Datelines

1940	On 11 December Cheltenham suffered its worst wartime bombing when Stoneville Street was hit. Six hundred were made homeless and twenty-three killed. Winter Garden demolished.
1941	Emergency feeding centres were set up in Cheltenham. Six children playing in Worcester Street were killed when they detonated an unexploded bomb.
1942	In July eleven people were killed in a bomb raid on Brunswick Street. Iron railings and gates disappeared all over town as scrap for the war effort. Fuel shortages meant that many families had a winter without coal. Fire watching of business premises became compulsory.
1943	More fire watchers were urgently needed. The freedom of the borough was conferred on Ald. Clara Winterbotham.
1944	Seven thousand evacuees arrived in Cheltenham following attacks on major cities by 'Doodlebugs' and V2 rockets.
1945	Street parties galore to celebrate the end of the war. Cheltenham's first prefabs went up at Priors Farm, followed by others at St Marks and the Reddings. The Lynworth estate was laid out.
1946	Cheltenham made application for county borough status, but was refused after opposition from the county council. A compulsory order was sought for the purchase of land at Hesters Way for housing.
1947	Blackbird, the last of the corporation's horses, went into retirement. Record blizzards and freezing conditions in January and February gave way to record flooding in March.
1948	One-way traffic was introduced to North Street, Albion Street, Pittville Street and the High Street.
1949	Cheltenham Festival of Literature was founded in 1949. Its artistic director was John Moore, the Tewkesbury-born author and broadcaster.
1950	Work began on the new Royal Well bus station at an estimated cost of £14,420. Plans were made to rebuild Pilley bridge, which was destroyed in the war.
1951	Princess Elizabeth visited Cheltenham. She cut the first turf for the Hesters Way estate. This was the wettest year since 1930 with 33in of rain.
1952	A record 417 council houses were built in the town. GCHQ moved to Cheltenham. Staverton Airport was released back into civilian use after its wartime military role.
1953	Sunday morning bus services began in Cheltenham. The estimate for Royal Well bus station was increased to £16,648.
1954	Industry expanded in the area with Dowty leading the way. The firm planned new factories at Arle Court and Ashchurch. The annual accounts of the company reported a profit of over £1 million, with a dividend of 33 per cent.

1955   Elm Street, Malvern Street, Worcester Street and Waterloo Street were demolished as part of the postwar slum clearance programme. The Opera House (Everyman) was bought by the borough council.

1956   Couples were forbidden from cuddling in Town Hall corridors on dance nights. Cheltenham voted £6,000 to buy Sandford Mill Farm for use as a fun fair site. George Dowty was knighted for services to aviation.

1957   Petrol rationing was introduced because of the Suez Crisis. To meet the demands of the expanding town, plans were made to increase Cheltenham's water supply from 5.5 to 7.5 million gallons a day at a cost of £1 million.

1958   The newly formed Cheltenham Civic Society expressed concern about demolition works and urged that the town's architectural heritage be safeguarded.

1959   Cheltenham's fire brigade moved to its new Keynsham Road headquarters.

SIX

Demolition Decades 1960–79

T he biggest swinger in '60s Cheltenham was the demolition man's hammer. Buildings that would be listed treasures today were reduced to rubble then. One of the most notable was the boys' Grammar School in the High Street. Many people will recall the imposing features of the building, which dated from 1889. Designed by local architects Knight and Chatters, the façade employed all the tricks of the Tudor Gothic style with buttresses, stone-mullioned windows, gargoyles, heraldic decorations, steep gables, a castellated roofline and even an octagonal turret that might have been plucked from a Walt Disney fantasy. Inside, though, the school was drab, gloomy and cramped. The decision was taken to construct a new building on the school's playing fields in Princess Elizabeth Way. The London firm of architects Chamberlain, Powell and Bon – designers of the Barbican and New Hall, Cambridge – was commissioned and the plans were agreed in 1962. It was a bold challenging and aggressively modern choice and controversy raged from the moment illustrations of the new school appeared. Despite this, work started in November 1962 and on 16 June 1963 the foundation stone was officially laid by the president of Corpus Christi.

Easter 1965 was move time, when pupils and staff left the ornate High Street premises for the stark new surroundings of Hesters Way. Two years later the town centre school was demolished, along with the adjacent Fleece Hotel and a row of characterful small shops. They were replaced by the less than lovely concrete range that squats on the spot now.

*   *   *

Opposite: The splendid Gothic fantasy façade of Cheltenham Grammar School disappeared in the knock-it-down frenzy of the 1960s.

Tudor Lodge, designed by S.W. Daukes, bit the dust in 1966.

One of Cheltenham's best examples of Victorian gothic domestic architecture was Tudor Lodge, which stood in The Park. This substantial house was designed by S.W. Daukes, the architect responsible for St Peter's church and St Paul's training college. It featured chimneys like chess pieces, tear-shaped roof tiles, decorated barge boards and thrusting balconies – and it was knocked down in 1966 to make way for a terrace of town houses.

'Knock it down' mania in '60s Cheltenham saw off over thirty pubs in the town, some with delightful names: the Dove and Rainbow in Burton Street, the Noah's Ark in St George's Street, the Prince's Plume in Princes Street, and Henrietta Street's Seven Stars. The Little Midland near Lansdown station in Gloucester Road was another casualty. Churches, such as St John's in Albion Street and Royal Well chapel, also succumbed to demolition fever.

There's no doubt that Cheltenham is the poorer for losing so many fine buildings in the '50s and '60s. And it's equally certain that the town is still suffering from what the

The New Club, a landmark building at the junction of Oriel Road and The Promenade was replaced by the Quadrangle. (*Brian Donnan Photography*)

planners allowed to be built in those architecturally barren decades. In 1965 Eagle Star acquired a large chunk of Bath Road, flattened it and erected the multi-storey tower that opened on 18 October 1968. Five years later the sedate, understated and well-proportioned New Club on the corner of Oriel Road and the Prom was cleared to make way for the Quadrangle office block.

*   *   *

Winchcombe Street was a higgledy-piggledy collection of small retail premises, housed in a variety of architectural styles until the early 1960s. Then between 1962 and 1964 the whole of the east side of the street was demolished to be replaced by bland concrete. One of the casualties was a landmark building occupied by Dunn's on the

Buildings on the east side of Winchcombe Street had to make way for a uniformity of bland concrete.

corner of Winchcombe Street and the High Street. The half-timbered, Swiss chalet-style shop featured a carved frieze over the window, the top section of which was in stained glass. When it was demolished a new Martin's Bank was built on the site, an unremarkable building except for its grasshopper trade sign over the doorway.

A more ancient architectural gem swept away in the 1960s was the Basket Shop. It filled the gap that is now the entrance to the car park between the Lower High Street and Swindon Road, and was a rare leftover from the distant days when Cheltenham comprised only the High Street. The Basket Shop was timber framed with a shingle roof of Cotswold tiles, and was already ancient when it was acquired by James Tinkler in 1816. He sold baskets, brushes and rope. If still standing, the little shop would be listed and cherished, and tourists would take photographs of it. In 1967, however, the word conservation hadn't been invented and down it came.

All of Pittville Street from the High Street to Albion Street was knocked down and the small, individual shops of retailers such as Barnett-Hutton ladies' wear, Blackburns,

Dunn & Co. occupied the Swiss-style building on the corner of High Street and Winchcombe Street from 1926.

Whites and Gordon Thoday fabrics were replaced by a glass and concrete terrace typical of the time.

Looking back to the '50s and '60s it's difficult to understand why architects and planners went out of their way to put up buildings that remain eyesores even today. If a design was wrong in scale, used aesthetically inappropriate materials, was undeniably ugly and out of sympathy with its surroundings, planning permission was assured and the building was up in no time. Even discounting appearances, these town-centre shops were ill conceived. Many of them have upper storeys that could provide accommodation, except that there's no separate entrance.

*   *   *

Dowdeswell viaduct crossed the valley on stiletto heels until falling victim to dynamite and hammer.

Leckhampton and Charlton Kings lost their railway stations in the '60s. As a guidebook of the time tells us, both were 'on the BR Western Regional line, which is used by people doing business at Andoversford, Notgrove, Bourton-on-the-Water, Stow-on-the-Wold, Kingham, Chipping Norton, Rollright, Hook Norton, Bloxham and Adderbury, beyond which the line joins the one (Paddington to the great towns of the Midlands) at Kings Sutton near Banbury'. Courtesy of Dr Beeching, the line ceased to operate on 15 October 1962. Three years later the track was lifted and the land on which Charlton Kings station in Cirencester Road stood was sold to become an industrial estate. The site of Leckhampton station was put to the same use. This meant that Dowdeswell viaduct, which tip-toed delicately over the valley below, became redundant and was thanked for its long years of excellent service with dynamite and bulldozers. Other stations to close were Malvern Road and St James's in St James's Square. The council acquired the large tract that had been Cheltenham's only terminus station with marshalling yards and sidings. It promised that the St James's site would be developed in a way that would benefit the town as quickly as possible. Apart from one or two office blocks being built there, which few would argue did much to benefit the town architecturally, the land stood derelict for the best part of four decades.

*　　*　　*

Strolling down the Prom towards Paris House in 1961.

A stroll around the town centre in the 1960s might have taken you to Paris House on the corner of Oriel Road and the Promenade, which was a booking office for the Black and White and other coach companies. Fine models were often displayed there – a motor bus, an ocean liner, a steam locomotive – made by a local craftsman named Deeks who lived in St George's Place.

The frontage of Gillam's stationery and fancy goods shop at 396 High Street would undoubtedly be listed today. Installed in August 1939 in the commercial Art Deco style, the façade was of black marble with lettering of chrome. It was pulled down in the '60s.

Fishmonger Olive's had two shops in town, one at the Strand end of the High Street, the other in Clarence Street on the corner of Post Office Lane. Both premises were open-fronted and presented their fishy wares on slabs of cold white marble, made the more chilly by liberal scatterings of crushed ice. Here you could buy flat, delicately spotted sole, eel-like huss, whelks struggling to climb out of their imprisoning bucket

The pros and cons of a Lambretta LD 150 are being discussed outside Williams & Co. motorcycle shop in Winchcombe Street a year or two before the building and others in Portland Place were pulled down.

(every so often an assistant ran half a lemon round the rim to keep the molluscs in their place), whopping cod with bulging eyes and rosy-hued lobsters with pincers and whiskers – and for a treat a pint of prawns.

'Take away' was not a term in currency in the 1960s. Instead people said 'chip shop', and the town centre was well served by practitioners in the fish frier's art. Among the best was Beard's, a Mecca for cod connoisseurs that stood in Pittville Street between the Masonic Hall and Williams cycle shop. If you were looking for exotic fare, you'd find not a sausage of it at Beard's. Not a pasty, chicken leg, or beefburger, come to that. The proprietors played to their strength, the production of perfect fish and chips, and eschewed fashionable fripperies, such as the spring roll. Then there was Poole's in the Lower High Street. Mr Poole originally had one shop (close to Dicks Corner), then his son joined the business and expanded into the unit next door. A chip off the old block, so to speak. Further out of town at the junction with Townsend Street was the

Montpellier Rotunda shortly after Lloyds acquired the building in the early 1960s.

Walrus chip shop. Edward Street, a spoke off the Norwood Arms roundabout, was the address of Prior's Norwood Fish Bar. Roman Road had a fish shop at about the same time as The Beatles had their first number one, then the owners relocated 200 yards up the incline to Gloucester Road, no doubt benefiting from the increased trade as passengers left Lansdown station in need of warmth and sustenance.

At the more fashionable end of town, Montpellier's most striking feature – then as now – was the Rotunda. This great tureen sat over the spa that J.B. Papworth designed for the entrepreneur Henry Thompson in 1825. When Lloyds Bank bought the building for £14,000 in 1961, the place was in a sorry state. A survey revealed that the 160ft diameter, 60ft high dome had dropped 3in and was sagging on rotted roof beams. Two tons of copper and another two of lead were removed in the restoration, along with more tons of ornate plaster. More excitingly, workmen discovered steps

Walk into WARD'S — the modern store

E. L. WARD LTD.   CHELTENHAM

beneath the floor that led to bricked-up passages, while more tunnels were discovered from another subterranean stairway. When the former ballroom beneath the rotunda was stripped, the walls were found to be mirror-lined. A final find was a mid-nineteenth century postcard in the lantern at the top of the dome.

*   *   *

For a time in the '60s it seemed that any long recognisable parts of town that weren't being knocked down were being closed down. A local institution that disappeared was Ward's department store. The firm was founded in 1901 by E.L. Ward, who came from Essex. He took over a general store, just inside the Lower High Street, called Stranger's, which stood on about the spot now occupied by the post office. With its name changed to E.L. Ward's, the new retail outlet boasted the saga-length opening hours typical of the time: 8 a.m. until 9 p.m. Mondays to Fridays, 8 a.m. until 11 p.m. Saturdays. By 1910 twenty staff were employed. The business prospered, and as adjacent premises fell vacant Ward's acquired them. A shop named Beckingsale's became part of the empire. Then the ear, nose and throat hospital moved from Edmondstone House in North Street and was duly converted into additional floor space, plus three staff flats, for the store.

After a major rebuild and refurbishment in 1923 Ward's address became 136–40 High Street. To celebrate its re-opening a four-page special supplement in the *Chronicle and Graphic* announced 'The opening of our commodious premises situated in the heart of Cheltenham's shopping centre, which marks another milestone of progress in the history of this extensive store'. Extensive it certainly was, with departments for furs, umbrellas and handbags, fancy goods, drapery, corsetry, gloves, hosiery, lace and more.

Another major rebuild took place in 1937, by which time Ward's had extended even further along the High Street to occupy the corner plot that is today Littlewoods. A feature of the new-look store was its island display windows, and right up to the time of closure the shop had a high reputation for presenting interesting and unusually dressed window displays.

By the time Ward's celebrated its fiftieth anniversary in 1951 over 100 staff were employed in twenty-six departments on three floors all connected by lifts, the criss-cross doors of which were opened and closed by operators in blue livery coats. Each December the entire basement became a wide-eyed wonderland for kids who queued patiently (or not) to see Santa in his grotto. In 1950 Ward's Father Christmas dandled 30,000 children on his knee over the festive period, at 6*d* a dandle.

E.L. Ward entered local politics, served twice as town mayor and was made an alderman. But before we leave his splendid store there are two more 'must mention' memories. First the cash whizzer. When you handed over your money at Ward's the assistant didn't put it in a till. Instead your coins were dropped into a brass cylinder and attached to an overhead wire. The assistant then pulled something like a lavatory chain

The Friends' meeting house, Portland Street – one of many buildings in town that were constructed from Webb's bricks and demolished for no good reason in the 1960s.

and the cylinder whizzed your money off to the cashier, who worked out the change and whizzed it back. And lastly there was Laz. There must be hundreds, perhaps thousands, of people who grew up in Cheltenham who had their portrait drawn in charcoal by this artist. Laz sat at the foot of the ground-floor staircase on Saturdays, and for a small sum would capture the likeness of your little loved ones on that sort of grey paper with flecky bits in it that you used to do potato printing on at primary school.

Ward's closed in 1967, and four years later the building was removed to make way for the store that is today home to Littlewoods.

*   *   *

The end of another era came when the long tradition of brickmaking in Cheltenham finished with the closure of Webb's works at Battledown. If you live in the Cheltenham area and your house was built before about 1970, there's a good chance the bricks came from Battledown Brick Works. The Town Hall, the former brewery in Henrietta Street, the General Hospital and many other landmark buildings hereabouts are constructed from Battledown's products, and for many years the firm was a major employer.

The enterprise was founded in 1897 when brothers Roland and Harold Webb bought the Battledown Brick and Terra Cotta Company from the Revd Arthur Armitage. This was a diversification for the brothers, who had inherited a thriving coal merchant's business based in Tivoli from their father. Imbued with the entrepreneurial thrust that typified Victorian industrialists, the brothers Webb soon began trading in gravel, sand, turf and lime. In a separate venture they also took leases on the Winter Garden and Montpellier Gardens. In the former they arranged Britain's first recorded indoor tennis tournament and the latter they developed into a nationally regarded venue for the same sport. But back to bricks. The 30 acre works site occupied Coltham Fields, that area of town bounded by Hales Road, Rosehill Street, Hay Road and Battledown Approach. Today Queen Elizabeth playing fields stand where the clay pits were and the industrial estate in King Alfred's Way stands on what was the works complex.

Backed by the Webbs and directors such as John Haddon (half of the well-known Cheltenham retailer Shirer & Haddon), the well-funded company invested heavily in new brick-producing plant, replaced the old steam-powered machinery with gas engines, installed gas-making facilities on site and generally upgraded the works. An extensive railway network was laid to shuttle clay and sand from the pits to the works and new kilns were built. Vast sheds appeared where millions of bricks were stacked to dry, and a 120ft high chimney became a new feature of the Cheltenham skyline. Soon 30,000 bricks were being produced a day. Very particular bricks too. The local clay was unusually hard, so to make it workable water was added along with 'grog', the technical term for a mix of ground, baked clay, ashes and sand. This gooey blend was then extruded in a continuous line, like icing being squeezed from a bag, and cut by wire into bricks measuring 4in × 3in × 9in ready for firing. Battledown's wire-cut bricks had six flat faces, distinctly different from mould-made bricks found in other parts of the country that had a 'frog', or recess. The advantages of the local product were greater structural strength and the need to use less mortar. The disadvantage was that they were more expensive to produce, which ultimately led to the firm's demise. Tiles were made as well, sand-faced roofing tiles reckoned to be the best in the country. There are hundreds, perhaps thousands, of houses all over Britain that sit to this day under roofs made from Battledown tiles.

At the works' gate was a curious plaque inscribed 'Webb Brothers – successors to King Alfred the Great' and a statue of the Saxon monarch. This alluded to researches conducted by one of the Webbs that suggested the ninth-century king employed Italian craftsmen to make bricks from Cheltenham clay. The King Arthur motif and proud (if fanciful) slogan added interest to the company's promotional materials.

Looking from the High Street end of Winchcombe Street towards the Gaumont (now Odeon).

Webb's bought all other Cheltenham brickmakers and by doing so acquired land in Pilford, Harp Hill, Cemetery Road and Tewkesbury Road, all of which was developed for housing. By 1907 Battledown was the only place producing bricks in town.

Between the wars Webb Brothers diversified again. Their Buckle Furnace Coke subsidiary supplied the commodity all over the country in the firm's own fleet of railway trucks to addresses that included Windsor Castle and St James's Palace. Their Bukalla Tea Company delivered 'Tea straight from Ceylon to the teapot', as the advertisements declared. Waste materials from the brickworks were used to lay clay tennis courts. And for a time another subsidiary manufactured firelighters . . . until the factory caught fire.

During the Second World War, when the firm had its own Home Guard platoon, Battledown worked flat out to keep up with demand as shadow factories, air raid shelters and forces' facilities were hastily constructed. Postwar the picture was less rosy. By then the London Brick Company, the largest brickmaker in the world, could supply its products more cheaply than any competitor to all parts of Britain via improved road

The Savoy Hotel.

communications. Battledown brick and tile making came to a close at the start of the 1960s, and in that decade the company's land was sold to Cheltenham Corporation. Webb Brothers went into voluntary liquidation in spring 1971.

*   *   *

Bolstered by an increasing student population, teenagers with a little money in their pockets and the end of National Service in 1960, Cheltenham developed a thriving music scene. At the start of the decade jazz was the new sound, which could be heard most nights of the week in venues such as the Rotunda, St Luke's Hall (then in Bath Road) and the swimming club at the old Alstone Baths in Great Western Road. Jazz fans favoured pubs such as the Star, Cat & Fiddle, the Gladstone Arms and Eight Bells, and coffee bars The Tiffin (Royal Crescent), Bar-B-Q and Waikiki Club (Montpellier), the Patio Snack Bar in the Strand and El Flamenco. But if you were In with the In Crowd, the place to see and be seen was a private house at 38 Priory Street, where a jazz fan named Jane Philby started an impromptu café-cum-party venue for local musicians in the basement.

Jazz was replaced by rock and pop. Pop packages became all the rage in the early '60s when diverse artists appeared on the same bill. One unlikely coupling to appear at the Odeon in Cheltenham double-billed cockney rockers Joe Brown and the Bruvvers with Rolf Harris. In 1962 pop stars who came to town included Helen Shapiro in a show compèred by Dave Allen, as well as Billy Fury, Mike Sarne, Marty Wilde and Jimmy Justice. Cliff and the Shadows played Cheltenham in 1962 and '63 and on the second occasion local filmgoers who'd recently seen *Summer Holiday* had the chance to hear Cliff, Hank and co. perform the tunes. The back-combed hair, massed mascara and breathy voice of Dusty Springfield came to town in November 1964. Also on the bill were Herman's Hermits, Brian Poole and the Tremeloes, Wayne Fontana and compère Johnnie Ball (father of Zoe).

And that, as they say, was entertainment until The Beatles arrived. John, Paul, George and Ringo took the Odeon stage – and the town – by storm on 1 November 1963. It was the month when 'She loves you' ousted fellow Merseysiders Gerry and the Pacemakers' 'You'll never walk alone' from top position in the charts and Beatlemania was at fever-pitch. On the bill with the mop-topped Fab Four were the Rhythm & Blues Quartet, the Vernons Girls, Frank Berry, the Brook Brothers, Peter Jay and the Jaywalkers, and the Kestrels. As was the way at the time, The Beatles played a short set of about half an hour. Anyone who was present will, no doubt, recall a good deal about the evening, but not the sound of the music. Screaming obliterated that. There was dancing in the aisles and jumping on the seats, and when the boys unplugged their VOX AC30s and left the stage it was littered with jelly babies thrown by adoring fans of George, who was said to be partial to them. After the gig The Beatles stayed at the Savoy Hotel in Bayshill Road, where, until only a few years ago, the guest book open at the page signed by the celebrities was displayed in a glass case. All that screaming and jumping and jelly-baby throwing were firmly denounced by some stalwarts of society, who were appalled by the notion of young people enjoying themselves. In his weekly *Gloucester Journal* column, the paper's padre vitriolically voiced the establishment view of John, Paul and co.'s performance in Cheltenham: 'A lot of youngsters who went did not go to hear them. They went to hear themselves. Even in that they probably failed, unless they had a specially supersonic top C scream, capable of rising above everybody else's corybantic display. . . . Having achieved their new sound, [The Beatles] are to be applauded for whatever work and skill is required, but the result, judged as music – well, it isn't.' Others thought differently. Within two weeks of their appearance at the Cheltenham cinema the Liverpool lads were at numbers one and two in the charts with 'I want to hold your hand' and 'She loves you', while at number twenty-four was Dora Bryan's 'All I want for Christmas is a Beatle'.

Local crimpers were quizzed on their thoughts about Beatle hair cuts. 'I think it's a disgrace, very unhygienic and looks absolutely ridiculous. We get very little demand for the style, if one can call it a style,' replied one. Another salon spokesperson reported: 'Before the war the eastern European peasants let their hair grow in a similar way, chiefly because they had no mirrors and therefore didn't know any better.' A third observed: 'We get a few boys asking for Beatle haircuts and those that do are either very young or not very bright.'

*   *   *

Those stern voices that denounced The Beatles were left almost speechless by the more subversive Rolling Stones, who were riding a peak of popularity when they came to Cheltenham's Odeon to play two sell-out concerts on Thursday 10 September 1964. Their first album was a huge hit on both sides of the Atlantic. The single 'Not fade away' reached number three in the UK pop charts in March. The next single 'It's all over now' became their first number one in July (the month that the Stones enhanced their reputation for forthrightness when they appeared on TV's *Juke Box Jury* programme). The EP 'Five by five', released in August, clocked up sales of half a million. And on the very day they appeared in Cheltenham, the sixth date of a thirty-seven-stop UK tour, the Rolling Stones were voted the most popular British group in a *Melody Maker* poll.

Not surprisingly, the atmosphere created by hundreds of fans who gathered outside the Winchcombe Street cinema before the show was electric. Many were there for hours in the hope of glimpsing Mick, Keith, Charlie, Bill and Brian (especially Brian) arriving. Marketing hadn't hijacked pop music in those innocent times. So on that September day in 1964 there were no mugs, jugs, T-shirts, tea towels, books, bedspreads, crockery or nick-nackery emblazoned with the Rolling Stones' logo (indeed, there wasn't a Rolling Stones logo then). The sole sop to commercialism was a man in a sports jacket who offered black and white A3 size photographs of the lads priced at 2*s* 6*d*.

Compèring 'The sensational Rolling Stones show' was Don Spencer. Such was the excitement inside the Art Deco auditorium that his announcements were drowned out by screaming. But no doubt he explained that the evening's merrymaking was to open with The Innocents, followed by Mike Berry and the Mojos. Then came an interval before the crescendo of anticipation rose via the Le Roys, Simon Scott and Inezz and Charlie Foxx to reach its frantic climax when the tousle-haired fivesome took to the stage. The crowd went crazy, as the *Echo* of 11 September 1964 reported: 'Police officers, security men, commissionaires and first aid men linked arms last night to prevent screaming fans from rushing the stage at both performances by the Rolling Stones at the Odeon Cinema, Cheltenham. One girl managed to clamber onto the platform, but was quickly hauled down. During their lively act the Stones were pelted with sweets and other objects as tokens of affection.' After the show 'Crowds of fans waited outside in front of the cinema, but the Rolling Stones slipped out the back way with a police escort and went off in their own car.'

The Rolling Stones with Cheltenham-born Brian Jones on the right.

Cheltenham fans laid a special claim to the Stones, because Brian Jones was a local lad. His parents were among the audience at the early show, as were many people who'd known him before he moved to London to seek and find fame and fortune. After Dean Close Junior School, Brian Jones went to Cheltenham Grammar in the High Street and played clarinet in the school orchestra. He also studied piano and performed in a duet at an open evening. His multi-instrumental talents added a freshness to early Rolling Stones records, on which he played guitar, piano, harpsichord, organ, dulcimer, sitar, chimes, and introduced many British pop fans to the sound of bottleneck guitar on 'Little red rooster'.

Brian Jones officially left the Stones on 8 June 1969. The following month he was found dead in the swimming pool of his home in Hartfield, Essex. An obituary by Dr Arthur Bell, headmaster of Cheltenham Grammar School, appeared in the school magazine:

Brian Jones was a new boy in the year I joined the school in 1953. He always seemed quite clever and he did in fact do quite well in his 'O' and 'A' level examinations, though nothing like as well as he might have done had he been attracted to an academic career.

When he left school to go to London to study Applied Optics (as was then expected) he certainly seemed indifferent to the prospect. What happened after that and how he came to be one of a well known group of 'Pop' stars others can describe and I cannot. The life brought wealth and a certain kind of fame. I do not know if it brought happiness – and I very much doubt it.

Brian Jones seemed to me to be essentially a sensitive and vulnerable boy, not at all cut out for the rough and tumble of the commercial world.

*   *   *

A pioneering venue for live pop groups in Cheltenham was the Grotto Club, as the skittle alley behind the Wheatsheaf pub in Old Bath Road was called on nights when the pins and balls were replaced by electric guitars and drums. The Grotto's brief period of popularity came to a close in 1966, partly because of complaints about rowdiness, but more because a club called the Blue Moon opened above Burton's in Cheltenham's High Street and became the new focus of live rock. The Who, the Small Faces, Rod Stewart, Elton John and Jimi Hendrix were among the acts who appeared at the Blue Moon on their way to international stardom.

*   *   *

Cheltenham Borough Council was formed when, as a result of the reorganisation of local government in England and Wales in April 1974, Charlton Kings Urban District Council merged with Cheltenham Municipal Borough.

Four years later the new authority published its Central Area Interim District Plan, which was a vision of how the town centre was to develop. Perhaps because of reaction to the Eagle Star tower in Bath Road and the Whitbread high-rise block in St Margaret's Road, the plan assured townspeople that permission for offices would be carefully controlled, with just one new office block of up to 100,000 sq. ft to be purpose built on the St James's station site. This was duly built and occupied initially by Mercantile Insurance, and gave few people grounds to believe that our architects and planners had learned anything by mistakes made in the previous two decades. The plan outlined that part of the St James's station site and all of the Athletic Ground in Albion Street were to be developed for housing by the private sector. The latter development went ahead, but nothing happened at St James's. Nothing happening at St James's remained a feature of the town for a long while to come. This was partly because of

The Plough Hotel was said to have one of the largest coaching yards in the country. By the 1960s much of it was a car park, today occupied by the Regent Arcade.

difficulties with the site, such as the presence of toxic waste, but the real barrier to development was the sheer scale and importance of the site. With no real certainty of what should be done with this prime chunk of real estate, the authorities tacitly agreed it was safer to do nothing – except create a new landscaped walk and park along the River Chelt adjacent to the site. That wasn't likely to cause much controversy.

If you were in the market for a house in the mid-'70s a glimpse down the property for sale columns would have revealed that at the Elm Farm development in Fiddlers Green Lane new three-bedroomed semi-detached houses with built-in garage were selling for £9,650. New Regency town houses at Sandford Park, with four bedrooms and gas central heating had a tag of £19,250, while at Hambrook Park, Charlton Kings, recently built four bedroomed, two bathroomed, detached houses with double garages could be yours for £21,500.

Other ideas were mooted in the Central Area Interim District Plan. A new shopping precinct was to be built on the Plough Hotel/Regent Street car park site and the intention was to keep the existing façade of the old hotel. New shopping facilities were

Portland Street from Warwick Place, early 1960s.

to be concentrated in or adjacent to existing shopping areas: in other words, out of town retail parks weren't quite the thing for Cheltenham, thank you. Improved facilities would be provided for tourists, including increased use of Pittville Pump Room, such as the costume museum which was opened – and later closed. Tourist information facilities were to be expanded, with signposting, town trails and specialist holidays. A new athletics track and multi-purpose sports hall would be built at Pittville. Improved public transport and cycle facilities were made a priority. Recognising that the town's architectural heritage had taken a bashing for some time past, the plan announced that a presumption against the demolition of listed and nineteenth-century buildings would be implemented. Then, in an attempt to address the town's often gridlocked centre, it was proposed that a short stretch of dual carriageway should be built between St Margaret's Road and Fairview Road. The road was indeed built – and to make way for it numerous nineteenth-century buildings were demolished.

* * *

The story of Charlton Kings being officially absorbed by Cheltenham was a saga that continued for eighty years. In 1894, by Local Government Board order, part of the civil parish of Charlton Kings was added to Cheltenham. Then in 1935 the County of Gloucester Review Order transferred a further section of Charlton Kings to its larger neighbour. But until the reorganisation of local government in 1974, Charlton Kings had its own elected council and officers who met in the Urban District offices at Lexham Lodge, Six Ways.

In about 1950 Charlton Kings council produced a small guide to the village, from which we learn that the population was then 6,034 and that one of the major issues being considered by the council was whether to install electric street lighting in the village. At that time visitors could arrive by train at Charlton Kings station. Another way to reach the village was by tram. Cheltenham's public tram service began in August 1901 and the extension to Charlton Kings came into operation on 28 March 1905. Tramcar nos 13 to 20 ran along the route, which was from Cheltenham High Street up London Road to Six Ways, then right into Copt Elm Road. That part of the ride must have been like a roller coaster, with its steep descent then rise to Lyefield Road West, on to Cirencester Road and then back to join London Road at the Holy Apostles junction. The last tram in service by the Cheltenham District Light Railway ran for the final time from Lansdown to Charlton Kings just after dawn on 31 December 1930.

Even after it officially lost its independent status Charlton Kings retained a separate character, as it does to this day. One of its secrets is Bafford Lane, where there was a mill in operation in 1585. The clutch of houses found in this delightful backwater include some that date from the seventeenth century. Poet Laureate Cecil Day-Lewis lived at Box Cottage in Bafford Lane. He moved to Cheltenham in April 1930 when he obtained a teaching post at the boys' college. The following year he bought Box Cottage and lived there until just before the Second World War. During his residency the cottage needed a new Cotswold-tile roof. To pay for it, Day-Lewis wrote *A Question of Proof*, which was published in 1935. This was the first in a series of twenty-three big selling novels featuring the detective character Nigel Strangeways, that he penned under the pseudonym of Nicholas Blake. In 1973 the *Echo* celebrated its centenary, and produced a special supplement to which C. Day-Lewis contributed this rhyme:

The Roar of Cheltenham

Of quiet charm and gentle ways,
In far off 1920 days;
But with the seventies peace no more,
The roar of traffic to the fore.

The Promenade – renowned afar,
Well loved part of Cheltenham Spa;
With restful seats and welcome trees,
Where one could spend an hour of ease.

The scene has changed and for the worse,
Continual traffic – what a curse;
Now, from those shady seats we see,
Just mechanised monotony.

Yes – cars of every size and make,
With outsize lorries in their wake;
A veritable race track too,
With no regard for me and you.

There still remains a quiet spot,
Which folk have learned to love a lot;
Montpellier Gardens – fine indeed,
A refuge in the hour of need.

Here – traffic-weary souls may find,
Their sanctuary, peace of mind;
Refreshment in a quiet way,
A pleasant item in the day.

The flowers and lawns, tended with care,
Produce a scene extremely fair;
Winged chestnuts, too, provide their charm,
And they are happy – free from harm.

Now, Cheltenham council play your card,
Ban traffic from that Promenade;
In doing so, you may be sure,
You will be blessed for evermore.

One of the most remarkable buildings in Charlton Kings was the Moorend Park Hotel. Built between 1835 and 1840 by a Birmingham businessman named Frind Cregoe Colmore to a design by John Buonarotti Papworth, the house looked like a grand Bavarian hunting lodge. It became a hotel in the 1920s, when it was advertised as being AA and RAC three star rated, standing in its own grounds of 14 acres, with

The URBAN DISTRICT of Charlton Kings

HISTORY & GROWTH

Moorend Park Hotel.

central heating, tennis court, putting green, lock up garages, twenty-five rooms, fifteen of them with private bath. Unbelievably, the building was demolished in 1979. Charlton Kings' other well-known hotel, the Lilleybrook (now called the Cheltenham Park Hotel) was part of the estate, which included a golf course, bought by Leckhampton Quarries just after the First World War. In 1922 it became a hotel and was called the Lilleybrook after the stream that runs nearby. Lilley was the old word for wild garlic, which still grows along its banks in abundance.

*   *   *

RMS *Queen Elizabeth* with decorative fittings by H.H. Martyn & Co.

Perhaps the most lamentable loss to the town's employment and economic scene at this time was the closure of H.H. Martyn, a company that played a major role in the development of industry in Cheltenham and Gloucestershire. In these days of specialisation it seems incredible that there was once a company that built aeroplanes, motor cars, fitted out ships, cast statues, produced stained-glass windows, made furniture, worked iron, carved stone, moulded decorative plaster . . . and much more. But all were part of Martyn's portfolio.

Herbert Henry Martyn established his company of art craftsmen in premises on the corner of College Road and the High Street in 1888. So immediate was the success of this venture that by 1900 the firm had attracted a skilled workforce of 200 from all over the country. Space was needed for further expansion. So when H.H.'s son Alfred took control, the company moved to a 12½ acre site at Sunningend, which is now Lansdown Industrial Estate. A large foundry was built at the new works, which soon received its first major commission. A team of eighty worked for three months to make the iron gates for London's Marble Arch. Weighing 40 tons and costing £3,000, the magnificent illustration of craftsmanship in iron incorporated over 10,000 hand beaten laurel leaves.

The firm was good at grabbing publicity opportunities. So when it received the Royal Warrant for decorative interior work in Buckingham Palace's Long Gallery and Windsor Castle, the potential for boosting its reputation was not overlooked. Subsequently orders were received that established Martyn's reputation worldwide: a stone pulpit for Brisbane cathedral, wood and plasterwork for the Maharajah of Indore's Lal Bagh Palace, carving and bronzework for the royal trains of King Carol of Rumania and King Farouk, and many more highly prestigious British commissions. Martyn's produced the cast iron and bronze frontage to Selfridges in Oxford Street, the speaker's chair and dispatch boxes in the House of Commons, the Cenotaph, Whitehall – all work that can be seen to this day, along with examples too numerous to mention in grand houses, the finest hotels and institutional buildings throughout the country.

By 1910 over 1,000 people were employed at Sunningend, making Martyn's the area's largest employer. Not content with mastery of its field on dry land, the company next ventured to sea and took to the air. First ships. Martyn's was responsible for fitting out over a hundred of the world's greatest ocean liners, including the *Titanic*, *Lusitania*, *Canberra*, *Queen Mary*, *Queen Elizabeth* and *QE2*. Then planes. During the First World War Martyn's began making military aeroplanes under contract, from which was born the Gloster Aircraft Co. As mentioned earlier, the company also diversified into car manufacture in the 1920s, and also built a motor scooter.

The firm continued to produce fine art and craft work right into the 1960s. It cast sculptures by Henry Moore, the bronze of Winston Churchill in London's Guildhall, and a statue of Robert the Bruce, which was unveiled by the Queen at Bannockburn in 1964. Martyn's probably represented the greatest concentration of art craftsmanship and trade skills in the country, but the demise of Britain's shipbuilding industry in the 1960s sounded the final death knell. The London furniture maker Maples, which had acquired a controlling interest in the Cheltenham firm during the 1930s, sold off Martyn's assets and closed the company in 1971. Its disappearance was a sad loss, but many made-by-Martyn's products still to be seen around the world are an enduring memorial to a company that was universally regarded as the best.

Craftsmen who completed their apprenticeships at Martyn's provided a pool of skilled labour for other businesses in the town. Cheltenham Caravans at Leckhampton was one of them. During the '50s and '60s the firm was a pioneer in the use of glass fibre moulded caravan bodies. This new material was seen on such models as the popular Clubman and Fawn. Its advantage was that construction was seamless, making rainwater leaks less likely. In the 1970s trading conditions became difficult for caravan makers. The oil crisis sent petrol prices skyrocketing, which largely killed the appeal of caravanning as a cheap holiday. Inflation was high, unemployment was high, then in the Budget of April 1975 VAT on luxury goods, which included caravans, was raised to 25 per cent. The affect of this hike was to add £400 to the selling price of a caravan. Within a week the proprietor, Cecil Gardner, announced that after fifty-three years in the town his company had gone into voluntary liquidation and was closing with the loss of thirty jobs. As the *Echo* reported: 'The men, some of whom have been with the company nearly 30 years, and most of whom are skilled craftsmen, immediately downed tools and left the factory to sign on at the Department of Employment.' It was an abrupt and sad end to a local firm that had taken the town's name far and wide.

The same could be said of Tilley's Crumpets. Following a century of production the Bath Road baker closed in June 1977, forcing seven men and thirty-seven women on to the dole after a long and unresolved dispute with the TGWU and the Bakers' Union.

A larger employer that closed in the '70s was UCAL, the United Chemists Association Ltd, which had its manufacturing centre in Corpus Street, off London Road. The company made hundreds of pharmaceutical products, which were sold exclusively through independent chemists across the country. Throughout the 1960s UCAL faced increasingly strong competition from bigger players in the pharmaceutical business, and a series of serious fires caused neighbouring residents to voice misgivings about living next door to large stores of volatile chemicals. Their fears were allayed when in 1972 UCAL was bought for £250,000 by Maccarthy's Pharmaceuticals, and soon afterwards production in Cheltenham ceased.

*   *   *

A curiosity to disappear in the early '70s was Lansdown Castle, a castellated, Victorian gothic house that stood at the junction of Gloucester Road and Lansdown Road. Cheltenham-born composer Gustav Holst named one of his earliest performed works after the curious building, which before its demolition was a shop.

In Clarence Street St Matthew's tower had been a cause of concern for some years. In the 1950s the broach spire that topped the town-centre landmark was taken down, then in 1972 the tower was lowered to its present height.

On the side of Winchcombe Street that wasn't flattened in the previous decade stood Drake's, which was founded in the town in 1888 and remained in business until 1978. At first a drapery store, Drake's branched into home fabrics and upholstery, then furniture. In the 1920s and '30s the shop pioneered the presentation of bedroom and lounge suites in room displays, so customers could see what that armchair looked like alongside this coffee table. Sounds simple now, but it was quite a breakthrough at the time. The shop boasted an impressive sign – protruding from the wall like a pub's – depicting the *Golden Hind*, an oblique reference to Drake.

Another well-known local department store, Shirers & Lance's, disappeared in 1979. The origins of the store went back to about 1833 when two employees of Cavendish House, Alexander Shirer and Donald McDougall,

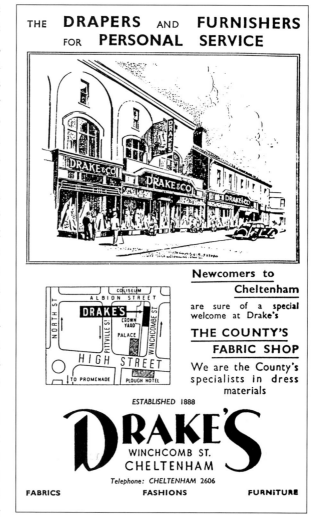

set up on their own in the drapery business, trading under the name of Shirer & Sons. The firm merged with another local retailer to become Shirer & Haddon. Then in 1937 it joined forces with a competitor, John Lance & Co., and the name over the shop doorway changed yet again, this time to Shirer & Lance's. The firm occupied most of the Colonnade, with departments on two floors. Shirer & Lance's also had a large, four-storey furniture store, which stood on the corner of Clarence Street and Well Walk. This nineteenth-century building was sold to the Cheltenham and Gloucester Building Society and demolished in 1974 to make way for the faceless office block that occupies the site today.

*   *   *

The former offices of Shirer and Lance's department store in Well Walk were acquired by the Cheltenham & Gloucester Building Society and pulled down in 1974.

Until the '70s most Cheltenham children learned to swim at the Alstone Baths. Crocodiles of kids from local schools, cossies wrapped in towels under their arms, arrived at the Great Western Road pools to front, back and breast stroke for all they were worth. Or at least to try. The big pool – 6ft at the deep end, 3ft at the other – boasted balconies along its length, where anxious parents sat on wooden benches and hoped their offspring would perform heroic feats on gala day. Beneath the balconies were changing cubicles, females to the left, males to the right. 'All possessions', as it said on the notice in the ticket booth, were 'left entirely at owner's risk'. The doors on the changing cubicles were barely deep enough to reach from knee to shoulder on most normal size people, a factor no doubt designed to discourage hanging about. Primary school children walked round the tiled edge of the big pool to the learners' pool, passing through the brief warmth and Cunard liner-style pipework of the boiler room. This was one of the great mysteries about the Alstone Baths. The boiler room was always like a sauna, while the water in the pools felt as if it was specially piped from Siberia.

Cheltenham's first municipal swimming facility – for such was the honour of the Alstone Baths – opened in June 1887. The new public amenity stood close to a centuries-old mill, the water wheel of which had been coaxed round by the tumbling River Chelt. The Cheltenham Swimming and Water Polo Club met at the Alstone Baths, where goals suspended from the ceiling were lowered for matches. A founding member of the club was Colin Lewis, who swam for Britain in the London Olympic Games of 1908. When the town's new public pools opened at Pittville the Alstone

Pittville swimming pools were opened by Queen Elizabeth the Queen Mother in 1971.

Baths were surplus to requirement. By then the place was run down and hardly a credit to the town. Closure came in 1975, then for a year or two the building became a DIY store. That was the end of a local landmark, one that was part of growing up for thousands of local people for whom those teeth chattering, chlorine smelling, whistle blowing swimming lessons at the Alstone Baths are now a memory.

*   *   *

During the summer of 1977 a large bough fell from one of the vast and spreading horse chestnuts that lined the Promenade. This prompted Cheltenham Borough Council to commission a report on the condition of the trees – and the results caused widespread

By the late 1970s it was time for the Prom's famous chestnut trees to bow out.

dismay. Tree Conservation Ltd, the company that carried out the survey, concluded that the ancient chestnuts should be felled. Planted in 1818 when Cheltenham's foremost thoroughfare was laid out, the stability of the trees was considered to be, at best, unpredictable. Referring to the bough that had fallen earlier in the year, the report commented: 'Similar failure of possibly massive branches is liable to occur with any of these over-mature horse chestnuts and it is virtually impossible to predict where or when this might happen.' The suggestion was made that replacement trees should be open crowned, such as planes, to allow a better view of the town centre architecture.

*   *   *

In the midst of these business closures and demolitions, the disappearance of crumpet and chemical factories and threatening chestnuts, the Queen's Silver Jubilee of June 1977 provided Cheltenham with an oasis of celebration. There were Silver Jubilee street parties galore. Colesbourne Road, Benhall, stole the march on the rest of town by staging its party on the Saturday before the official Jubilee holiday. Barriers closed the road to traffic from early afternoon until late evening, and seventy-four local children sat at trestles in the middle of the road to tuck into cakes and jelly. Photographs in the local press captured the fun and games at similar gatherings all over town. One of the largest was at Clyde Crescent. This was attended by families from all over Whaddon and Lynworth, where a high spot of the day was the hotly contested knobbly knees competition for dads. Charlton Kings Infants' School pushed the royal barge out with a day of music, dancing and a re-enactment by pupils of the Prince of Wales's investiture. Children sang two Jubilee songs, especially written for the day by Marion Brunskill, a teacher at the school. The percussion band performed a Jubilee tribute composed by another teacher, Geoffrey King. But the occasion wasn't entirely trouble free. Shortly before Jubilee day workers at the Royal Mint went on strike, and consequently the commemorative 5s coins were in short supply. To offset the disappointment, many children in town were given a Jubilee mug instead.

*   *   *

Another great cause for celebration, for cricket fans at least, was 'Mike Procter, the great South African all-rounder, whose centuries and fast bowling largely helped to make the 1973 Cheltenham Festival the most successful since the war, with two championship wins and a crushing John Player League victory over Warwickshire'. So wrote the *Echo* of a player – and later Gloucestershire captain – who led the county through a glorious decade. At the Cheltenham Festival in 1977 Procter scored a century before lunch against Worcester. There was a curious episode in the game. Basil D'Oliveira and the Gloucestershire bowler Brian Brain were driving to the game together in a car that broke down; consequently they weren't at the College ground for the start of play. Rather than hold things up, the home side went in to bat and proffered Jim Foat to field for Worcester until Mr D'Oliveira arrived. Mike Procter was just about into double figures when he skied a ball towards his team-mate, temporarily on loan to the opposition, on the boundary. The unfortunate Foat was now faced with an approaching ball and a ticklish dilemma. Should he catch the ball in the true spirit of the game and dismiss his own captain, or. . . . Well, let's say that Jim Foat narrowly missed a difficult chance, probably because the sun was in his eyes.

*   *   *

By the '70s Cheltenham could hardly be described as prim and proper as it once had been, but a hint of its reputation from a former time re-emerged when a soft porn French film, *Emmanuelle*, was showing at the ABC cinema. The manager, Clive Jones, taped over the more racy bits of the publicity posters so as not to offend visitors to the town, or pupils at the nearby Ladies' College. This delightfully coy and public-spirited act was reported in the national press.

While on the subject of the ABC, which stood on the corner of the Promenade and St George's Road, *The Sting* (1974) starring Paul Newman was the most successful film ever shown at the cinema. It ran for six consecutive weeks, was screened 120 times and

The Opera House became the Everyman in 1960.

Cavendish House before the elegant 1820s frontage was replaced in 1964 by what's there now.

played to 30,389 patrons. To celebrate its fortieth anniversary the ABC threw open its doors in 1979 and gave guided tours to anyone who was interested, as many people were. Chief projectionist Peter Massie revealed the secrets of his profession to visitors, who also had the chance to meet Rose Peters, who lived in Baker Street and who had been a cleaner at the cinema almost from its opening in 1939.

Datelines

1960   The Opera House closed for refurbishment and re-opened as the Everyman Theatre. At the end of the year the Municipal Offices were gutted by fire. The inferno swept from the ground floor to the roof, but the façade remained undamaged.

1961   In the national census Cheltenham's population was 71,968.

1962   It was announced that the Cheltenham to Kingham railway line was to close. Disc parking was given the go ahead in town and motorists were issued with a revolving cardboard clock to display in their vehicles. Cinema names changed. The Gaumont became the Odeon, while in the Prom the Regal was renamed the ABC.

1963   The Daffodil cinema became a bingo hall.

1964   Long-discussed plans for a new public swimming pool hit a snag when a covenant was discovered preventing development on the proposed Sandford Park site. Lilleybrook golf club bought its 103-acre course for £18,000. Cavendish House was given a new façade, replacing the original frontage that dated from the 1820s.

1965   More cuts to the railway service were announced as a result of the Beeching report. Cheltenham's St James and Malvern Road stations were earmarked for closure.

1966   A Scots piper played a lament from the platform as the last train from London pulled into St James's station. Complaints were voiced that the property market had stagnated because the council was slow to publish its town centre plan.

1967   A six-week public enquiry examined options for the redevelopment of central Cheltenham. The resulting plan was rejected. Driver-operated buses were introduced. H.H. Martyn & Co. won a £250,000 contract to provide panelling, ceilings and fittings for the new Cunard liner QE2.

1968   With an eye to the future, Cheltenham corporation bought the St James's station site for £250,000 and promised its early development. The Eagle Star tower block in Bath Road opened.

1969   Dean Close School opened fifteen places to 'serious girl students'. A town centre landmark, the New Club – at the junction of the Prom and Oriel Road – was bought by developers for £110,000. Cheltenham's town clock, which projected from the gable of Tesco's on the corner of the High Street and Church Street, was removed after fire engulfed the supermarket.

1970   Cheltenham police headquarters moved from Crescent Place to Lansdown Road.

1971   New public swimming pools at Pittville were opened by Queen Elizabeth the Queen Mother. Holy Apostles, Charlton Kings, suffered a serious blaze; but for the prompt action of the fire brigade the church might have been lost altogether.

1971   Cotswold Hills Golf Club bought 150 acres of farmland at Ullenwood.

1972   The Technical High School moved from Gloucester Road to newly built premises in Warden Hill Road, and was renamed Bournside Comprehensive. Closure was announced of R.L. Boulton & Sons, the Bath Road firm of stone sculptors responsible for the statue of Edward VII at Montpellier, stonework in many local churches and war memorials all over the country. Cheltenham's Christmas lights were heralded as among the best in the country for any provincial town. The cost of staging the illuminated show was £5,200 and the bill was met jointly by the Chamber of Commerce and the town council.

1973   Cheltenham's Odeon was converted to a triple-screen cinema. Dowty mining equipment received a £12 million order from China. The long awaited second town-plan proposals for Cheltenham were greeted with widespread opposition. It was reported that Cheltenham ambulances carried 260,000 patients and travelled 1,697,627 miles during the year.

1974   The Holst Birthplace Museum opened. The Countryside Commission moved into John Dower House, Clarence Street. *Bonnie and Clyde* was the final film shown at the Coliseum before the Albion Street cinema became a bingo hall.

1975   A capacity audience of 3,500 at the College field watched the Cheltenham Searchlight Tattoo, with massed military bands and a firework spectacular.

1976   St James's church in Suffolk Square became redundant and was converted into St Philip & St James's parish hall.

1977   The Queen's Silver Jubilee. There were street parties in celebration all over town.

1978   The centenary of the Cheltenham Cricket festival. Drake's of Winchcombe Street closed.

1979   Shirer and Lance's, one of the town's longest established department stores, shut up shop for the last time.

SEVEN

Catching Up with the Twentieth Century 1980–99

The largest single development in Cheltenham during the 1980s was the Regent Arcade. Costing £23 million, the shopping mall was built between 1982 and 1984 on the site of the forty-five bedroomed Plough Hotel, an ancient coaching inn that fronted on to the High Street, as well as the yard and car park behind it. Considerable opposition to the scheme was voiced and 20,000 signatures were collected by people who didn't want the development at any price. Campaigners staged a photographic exhibition entitled 'The Rape of Cheltenham' to illustrate how the town had suffered in the past at the hands of 'bureaucratic and speculative development at the expense of public opinion and sensible conservation values'. Despite these misgivings, the 185,000 sq. ft arcade with its 78 shops and parking for 540 cars was officially opened by the Princess Royal in May 1985.

Although established as a cultural centre and host town for arts festivals, Cheltenham was poorly served by venues at which local artists and craftspeople could show their work. Consequently plans were mooted to transform the Victorian grain warehouse in Winchcombe Street owned by agricultural merchants W.J. Oldacre into a centre for the performing and visual arts. A trust was formed by local volunteers to convert the building into a theatre and exhibition space where classes and concerts could be held. The Axiom Art Centre was the result. As is often the way with such ventures, the Axiom lurched permanently at the brink of financial ruin, but succeeded in staging shows of paintings by schools and other groups. It also provided one of the very few venues in town where aspiring rock groups could be given a hearing. The centre closed abruptly in February 2000 amid allegations of fraud, leaving young musicians with nowhere to plug in their amplifiers.

The Plough Hotel.

Another building that was given a new role was Leckhampton Court. After years of crumbling decline, the grand old building that was once home to lords of Leckhampton manor was acquired by the Sue Ryder Foundation and became a hospice.

The Promenade lost a landmark in the mid-'80s when the ABC was pulled down. More than just a cinema, this picture palace was a gateway to the glamour of the movies. The fantasy began the moment you crossed the threshold and entered the foyer, spacious and palatial, from which rose a sweeping staircase that might have been plucked from a Busby Berkeley production. Once climbed it opened on to a mezzanine. At either end were heavy, padded doors that gave entry to the circle where the eye was greeted by a glorious expanse of silver screen Art Deco. In the auditorium were chandeliers suspended from the heady heights, decorative pilasters and plasterwork, hints of Egyptian tombs and motifs of the orient. All was splendid and sumptuous. The last cinema to be built in Cheltenham (it opened for business on

2 January 1939), the Regal occupied the spot that had previously been the Imperial Spa pump room and was the work of well-known cinema architects W.R. Glen and L.C. Norton. Despite its undoubted grandeur and impressive scale, audiences at the new cinema were not entertained between films by a multi-consoled, mighty Wurlitzer. The Regal, which in 1962 was renamed the ABC, never had an organ.

Closure came on Saturday 14 November 1981. The final show was a double bill of *Kentucky Fried Movie* and *The Other Cinderella*, two entirely unmemorable films that ushered out an era. Sold to developers for £400,000, the ABC fell victim to the swinging ball in 1985. For a day or two the Prom façade was left standing, while the back of the building had been razed. This meant, curiously, that from Royal Well you could see into the once gorgeous interior, the ornate features knocked about, the fantasy reduced to rubble. Some of the red, plush, swing-back seats were taken to the New Olympus Theatre in Gloucester where they're still serving their purpose. But precious little else was saved.

There was heated debate over the fate of the former cinema site, which became something of a test case on the direction Cheltenham should take in the future. The development company that owned the plot put forward radical plans to erect an ultra-modern office block faced in smoked glass. The design was bold, starkly modern and altogether out of keeping with its neighbours in the Prom. Surprisingly, perhaps, some members of the conservation lobby argued in its favour on the grounds that something uncompromisingly new was preferable to Regency pastiche. Councillors, however, voiced opposition to the scheme. One said it must have been designed 'in a lunatic

The Regal cinema, later the ABC, screened its final film in 1981 and was demolished to make way for Royscot House.

After costly architectural mistakes made in the 1950s, '60s and '70s, Cheltenham has tended to favour Regency replica for its landmark buildings. This is The Broadwalk, which completed Imperial Square.

asylum'. Another thought the plan 'Brilliant. But not in the Promenade.' A third declared it 'a big load of rubbish'. In response, the boss of the development company (who may have been making an attempt on the world arrogance record) said the designs for the Dallas-style office block were too technical for councillors to understand. A compromise was suggested by the borough's planning committee, that the cinema be replaced with a building that was period replica on the Prom side and glass and concrete on the Royal Well side. The result was Royscot House, completed in 1987 at a cost of £3 million.

A further change to the face of the Prom came at about the same time when, as previously mentioned, many of the old chestnuts were felled for reasons of safety. This was a disastrous decade for the town's trees. By the 1980s Dutch elm disease had destroyed 4,500 specimens in and around Cheltenham, and other trees were lost because of birch bark, sooty bark, oak wilt and other arboreal nasties.

The debate over the future of the ABC site illustrated that people had strong views about what the showcase parts of town should be like. Often these opinions were voiced in the negative, with individuals and groups being quite certain about what was inappropriate, though less willing to commit themselves to what was suitable. Predominantly, though, from the Royscot House episode on, Cheltenham chose Regency pastiche as the way forward for its leafy parts. The Broadwalk was completed in this style, giving Imperial Square a finished symmetry it lacked before. In nearby Montpellier Spa Road a similar Regency look-alike terrace completed in the 1990s was equally successful, and both developments had the advantage of providing residential accommodation at the heart of Cheltenham.

Voices in the town were raised not only over large-scale issues, such as landmark buildings, but also over small details, such as statues. Never overburdened with statues, the town centre scene suddenly changed when a 10ft tall rabbit appeared in Imperial Gardens. The bronze bunny was complemented by a flock of metal sheep in the walled garden behind the Town Hall and, most enigmatic of all, a minotaur with its arm round a hare, which took up residence in the Prom. All were the work of Cirencester sculptor Sophie Ryder, and were cast in Gloucestershire at Chalford. The bronze bunny hopped it and the sheep moved to pastures new, but the minotaur and hare stayed, to the vociferous annoyance of some. Objections were made on grounds that the 2½ tonne figures were pagan, that they were too graphic in certain details and much else. But thanks to a group of enthusiasts who campaigned to raise £50,000 to keep the statue in town, the hare and minotaur became a permanent feature of the Prom. While controversy raged about whether or not a statue was suitable for this fashionable part of Cheltenham, an initiative that received far less publicity was launched to improve housing and environmental conditions in the Lower High Street. The ten year, £1.3 million scheme designated this neglected part of town a neighbourhood renewal area.

Not all replica Regency developments were as pleasing to the eye as those fronting on to Imperial and Montpellier Gardens. In The Park a block of flats, apparently designed with a 6in soil pipe as the focal point of its façade, appeared on ground that had previously been occupied by the Park Place Hotel. Over a late summer weekend in the '80s a fascinated crowd watched as the hotel was reduced to rubble by a large iron ball suspended on a chain from the jib of a crane, like a Hammer Horror game of conkers. By the time it was razed the Park Place Hotel, previously the Majestic, was not at its pristine best. But there must be numerous local people who recall the establishment with fond memories, as the venue for a wedding reception, anniversary, or function. First opened in 1932, the hotel stood on the corner of Park Pace and Ashford Road. The building was originally an imposing town villa of four storeys with a grand entrance up steps covered by a pediment on columns dating from the 1830s. As a hotel it was an immediate success and within two years vast alterations took place. An annexe to the original house more than doubled its size, and then a fifth floor was added with a flat roof. This concealed the former Victorian house behind an Art Deco façade. Inside, the fixtures and furnishings were Art Deco too, and very modern they must have seemed to guests who came after the official opening by His Worship the

Hotel Majestic, later Park Place Hotel.

Mayor of Cheltenham, councillor E.L. Ward (owner of the High Street department store) in May 1934. The cocktail bar was a popular meeting place until the hotel's demise and bristled with Art Deco features. There was even a ritzy white piano in the corner, sometimes encouraged into tune by an ivories tickler in white DJ.

*   *   *

Cheltenham's sixty-year position at the hub of Britain's coach network came to a close in 1985 when the Black & White coach company was taken over by the Cheltenham & Gloucester Omnibus Co. The following year the coach station in St Margaret's Road, which employed about 300 people, became redundant when the Cheltenham interchange was replaced by others in Bristol and Birmingham.

In peak season some 300 coaches left Cheltenham at 2 p.m. each day bound for destinations near and far. When the Black & White began a service to Paris complaints were received about the uniform worn by drivers of black trousers, black jacket with white piping, the company's emblem on each lapel and peaked cap fronted by the B&W logo. The French authorities said it was similar to the outfit members of the SS wore when Paris

Opposite: Two and a half tonnes of controversy – the hare and minotaur statue by Sophie Ryder.

The derelict Black & White coach station site in St Margaret's Road.

was occupied by the Nazis and it upset people. Not wishing to offend, the coach company re-equipped drivers crossing the Channel with simple grey flannel jacket and trousers.

After its closure the former site of the Black & White coach station became a temporary car park. Temporary, that is, in the Cheltenham sense. Various developments were mooted, plans were put forward and revoked, a Stakis hotel was almost built, but then wasn't. If the Black & White coach station is developed as quickly as St James's railway station, it could be a car park for decades to come.

* * *

During the 1990s Pate's Grammar became one of the first schools in the country to opt out of local-authority control and gain grant-maintained status. This development came at a time when the school's 1960s building was in a poor state of health, having fallen victim to concrete cancer. In 1996 the ailing landmark building at Hester's Way – square, squat and copper domed – was reduced to rubble and replaced by a more modest building in the contemporary superstore style.

Another building to disappear was the Lansdown Inn, Gloucester Road, which Whitbread planned to replace with TGI Friday's, an application that met with a lively response from borough councillor Mrs Jacky Thorpe. 'This is going to be an up-market, yuppie type place, attracting Porsches and Jaguars, which they drive in a reckless way,' she told members of the planning committee. The American eatery went ahead.

* * *

The grammar school building at Hesters Way lasted just thirty years before falling victim to concrete cancer.

In the early '80s the sole remaining private residence in the Prom was converted to commercial use. This was also a time when the few small shops left in the town centre that began in business to serve the people who lived there fell by the wayside. The year 1985 saw the demise of C.J. Morgan & Co., the Queen's Circus grocery store that had supplied the everyday needs of town centre residents since 1872 (the premises had been a food shop since 1838). A similar reminder of old Cheltenham disappeared when Whittern's closed its doors for the last time. A little out of town, Whittern's exhibited olde worlde charms and stood at the corner of Suffolk Road and Suffolk Place. Loose tea was kept in large glass jars and weighed out on scales. Provisions were displayed on shelves, with other goodies stored in wooden fixtures behind the counter. Blue bags for your washing could be had. And while the shopkeeper gathered the groceries, the customer was invited to take a seat.

For over a century the larger than lifesize manikin of a Gordon Highlander, complete with kilt, bearskin and sporran, stood guard outside Frederick Wright's, the High Street tobacconist. Cheltenham's famous tartan wearer disappeared to London when Frederick Wright's closed in 1987. Then he came up for auction in 1990, was bought by the grandson of the chap who founded Frederick Wright's, and now you can visit him in Cheltenham museum.

Madame Beatrix Taylor's splendid millinery establishment survived as Cheltenham's (and probably Gloucestershire's) only specialist hat maker until the mid-1980s. It stood at the Strand end of the High Street adjacent to Skiff & Hawkins, a ladies' fashion shop that disappeared at about the same time.

Cavendish House closed its food hall in 1997, having shut its silver-service restaurant some while before, but perhaps the final vestige of a long gone Cheltenham

Once a familiar figure outside Frederick Wright's High Street tobacconist shop, the Gordon Highlander manikin now resides in the town's museum.

disappeared when Madame Wright's left the Little Promenade. Until the last this gown shop, with its glorious Art Deco façade, continued to close on Wednesday and Saturday afternoons as it had for many years. Nothing so common as a price tag was ever to be seen in the window of Madame Wright's. It was plainly too genteel for the 1990s.

Far less well ordered was the Aladdin's cave of a shop on the corner of Montpellier Walk and Montpellier Spa Road, which closed following the death of its owner Ron Summerfield. The eccentric antiques collector was reluctant to sell anything and consequently the premises were choc-a-bloc with accumulated nick-nackery. But the shop was only part of the story. Mr Summerfield's home in Bayshill Road was also filled to the picture rails with artefacts and pictures collected over a lifetime – and there was a barn storing thousands more favoured items in Derbyshire. When he died of a stroke on Good Friday 1989, ambulance staff called to his home were unable to make their way up the stairs because of all the clutter, and Mr Summerfield had to be lowered down to the

Eccentric antiques collector Ron Summerfield did his best to prevent customers buying anything from his shop on
the corner of Montpellier Spa Road, but bequeathed a valuable collection of paintings to the town's art gallery.

ambulance on a winch from the upstairs window. Much of his lifetime collection was split in an auction that took some months to conclude and raised £8 million. But he bequeathed a treasured selection of paintings and objects to Cheltenham's museum and art gallery. He also set up a trust fund prior to his death to benefit his favourite charities.

Cheltonian Sir Ralph Richardson died in 1982. The actor-knight was born on 19 December 1902 at 11 Tivoli Road – an event now commemorated with a blue plaque fixed to the wall of the well-proportioned town villa. His father taught art at the Ladies' College, but by 1907 the marriage had broken up and Ralph left town to live with his mother in Sussex. His first job was as an office boy with an insurance firm, but he was drawn to the stage and managed to find small parts with a number of repertory companies. Richardson's career took off in 1925 when he moved to the Birmingham Rep and worked with Laurence Olivier. The two became lifelong colleagues and friends. Major West End roles followed and brought widespread public acclaim.

During the '30s Richardson and Olivier were regarded as the two leading Shakespearian actors in the country, but they also found the time to make films. Between 1932 and '39 the Cheltonian actor made fourteen appearances on the silver screen, including the role of British gung-ho adventurer Bulldog Drummond. Other starring movie roles included *Things to Come*, based on the book by H.G. Wells, and *South Riding* from the novel by Winifred Holtby. Both were produced by Alexander Korda. Ralph Richardson's TV debut came in 1939 when he appeared in *Bees on the Boatdeck*, a drama by J.B. Priestley. When war came he served in the Fleet Air Arm and rose to the rank of Lieutenant Commander – as well as playing roles in five propaganda films for the government. Richardson and Olivier joined forces once more when hostilities ceased by becoming directors of the Old Vic – an association, according to *The Times*, that 'once more brought the English theatre into an era of great acting'.

*   *   *

GCHQ hit the headlines in 1982 when Geoffrey Prime, who worked at the government agency as a linguist, admitted that he'd been spying for the Russians for more than a decade. He was jailed for thirty-eight years. The usually low-profile establishment was in the news again when the government announced plans to ban trade unions at GCHQ in the interests of national security. Outraged unions launched a campaign against what they saw as an attack on civil rights, and a national rally was organised by the TUC at which its general secretary Len Murray addressed a packed meeting in Pittville Pump Room. (In 1997 the Labour Government allowed unions back at GCHQ after a thirteen-year ban.) While all this was underway the more mundane issue of accommodation was being discussed. The twin site operations at Benhall and Oakley were expensive to maintain and it was felt that a single location would be more efficient. Various proposals were put forward, but in the end it came down to a choice between

Benhall or Brockworth. Cheltenham held its breath while the decision was being made. Only a few years before the Cheltenham and Gloucester Building Society had upped sticks and left the town for a new headquarters at Barnwood. To lose GCHQ the same way would be a blow, not only to employment, but to the prestige of the town.

There were sighs of relief when Benhall was announced as the chosen site, and work began on the Doughnut, as the football stadium-like building was soon dubbed, in spring 2000, when a consortium comprising the construction company Carillion, the security organisation Group 4 Falck and British Telecom won the tender to build, maintain and manage the new home for GCHQ. This was among the largest private finance initiatives in Europe. The deal was that the consortium shouldered the capital cost of £330 million, with the promise that GCHQ would rent the serviced complex for a sum of £800 million spread over thirty years. The plan also stated that Oakley would be sold off and 500 new houses plus a supermarket built there, with a further 300 houses being built on part of the Benhall site.

*   *   *

Back in the town centre the process of pedestrianisation, which began in 1977 when the Strand was paved over, continued during the '80s and '90s. Traffic was banned from the High Street between Winchcombe Street and Pittville Street, along with part of Regent Street. A section of the Prom followed suit.

The Spa Shuttle, nicknamed the 'Noddy Train', was considered by some a far-sighted attempt to address the town's traffic problems. Others said it was a waste of money. The others won the day and the trains disappeared from the town centre.

In an attempt to alleviate the town's parking problems, a scheme was proposed to burrow out 120 car spaces beneath the tennis courts in Montpellier Gardens. A £1,500 feasibility study was commissioned by the borough council's public works committee, and presumably concluded that the scheme wasn't feasible as it didn't happen. Instead the town's first multi-storey car park rose in Albion Street in 1982.

The traffic problem that Cecil Day-Lewis described in his rhyme about Cheltenham continued to dog the town. One-way systems came and went, and other action was taken, but this failed to address the cause of the problem – contemporary traffic volumes using yesteryear's road plan. A radical attempt to address the issue arrived in the late '90s when three Spa Shuttles took to the town centre. These 'Noddy Trains', as the shuttles soon came to be called, were bought at a total cost of £429,000 to provide a free ferry service to travellers around the town centre/Montpellier/Pittville areas. The annual running costs were £250,000. Some saw the gas-powered road trains as a far-sighted attempt to address the problems of traffic congestion and pollution. Others felt the Shuttles made the problem worse by reducing the speed of vehicles in their wake to a snail's pace. The greatest objection, however, was cost, especially when the hard-up council announced draconian cut backs. Earmarked for the axe were the Holst Birthplace Museum, Pittville's Costume Museum, hanging baskets, Town Hall concerts, the Playbus, Christmas lights, the 'Civic Amenity Centre', as the council tip is known. Amid the public outcry the council commissioned an opinion poll, which revealed that people in Cheltenham thought the best way to cut costs was to sell off the Noddy trains. They were withdrawn in September 1999, sold to a German theme park for £217,000, and Cheltenham's traffic problems were left intact. The voice of objection to the Spa Shuttle had a familiar tone. It had been raised not long before when the hare and minotaur statue appeared, and could be heard on most occasions when the tree-lined parts of town were threatened with anything new.

*   *   *

For a brief spell in March 1990 the town centre was devoid of all traffic, not because of any action by the highways department, but because of the Conservative Party's Central Council two-day conference. Cheltenham's centre was a no-go area when the tightest security operation ever seen in town was mounted. Most of Imperial Square was cordoned off and the gardens around the Town Hall were patrolled by officers with dogs. Look-outs were positioned on rooftops and even the drains were closely inspected. One of the main themes discussed by delegates was the party leadership, though Mrs Thatcher and her supporters denounced rumours of a challenge. Before the year was out, however, Michael Heseltine made a bid to oust the Iron Lady. She resigned after failing to win outright in the first ballot, and John Major became prime minister.

Tory turmoil at national level was reflected locally when the choice of Birmingham-born barrister John Taylor as the town's prospective candidate for the general election prompted racist remarks from a member of the Cheltenham Conservative Party. In the 1992 general election, Liberal-Democrat Nigel Jones won the Cheltenham seat.

*   *   *

In 1981 the biggest athletics event ever staged in Cheltenham took place when over 1,000 runners hit the road in the People's Half Marathon. The starting pistol was fired by champion jockey Terry Biddlecombe and athletes set off from Prestbury Park. The 'Crack Cancer' event raised thousands of pounds for the cobalt unit at Cheltenham General Hospital.

The Prince of Wales stadium opened the same year at Pittville. To celebrate the new facility a floodlit cricket match between Gloucestershire and Australia took place with a guest appearance by the legendary fast bowler Denis Lillee. Cheltenham RFC played their first game of the season against Harlequins at the stadium.

Amateur jockey Jim Wilson struck gold in March 1981 when he became the first non-professional rider since Dickie Black on Fortina in 1947 to win the Cheltenham Gold Cup. Jim's day job was helping injured and lame horses back to full strength at his equine swimming pool at Ham, Charlton Kings. But when he and his brother Robin inherited a race horse named Little Owl from their aunt, they thought they'd try their luck by entering the biggest race in steeplechasing.

No gallery of local sporting heroes would be complete without mention of Cheltonian ski jumper Eddie 'The Eagle' Edwards, who finished well behind the field in the 1988 Calgary Winter Olympics, but won the hearts of millions for having a go.

The weather was generally kind to Cheltenham's cricket festival during the '90s and the event grew from strength to strength with good crowds. By the end of the decade hospitality marquees surrounded pretty well half the playing area, restricting the view for the ordinary paying public, but helping to ensure the financial success of the festival. Like almost every other sport, cricket had become more of a business and less of a game, but even so Cheltenham's festival managed to maintain something of the atmosphere of a village game.

In the second half of the same decade the town's football team, the Robins, enjoyed a fairytale rise to success orchestrated by their manager, Cheltenham-born Steve Cotterill. At the start of the '90s the club was in such a dire financial plight that every player in the side was put on the transfer list in a desperate effort to raise cash. The average crowd at Whaddon Road was 200–300, and it looked as though the club might lose the ground and the site become a supermarket. Then Steve Cotterill came on the scene and provided three things that the Robins had been lacking for a long time: continuity, a strong sense of direction and inspiration. This proved a successful blend,

Inside

Tanks for a top wedding

Price 30p

GLOUCESTERSHIRE ECHO

ROBINS Victory Parade SPECIAL

Tel. 01242-271900 | The outlook: onwards and upwards | Monday, May 3rd, 1999

Picture: Simon Hadley 991620/b/28

CONGRATULATIONS TO CHELTENHAM TOWN FC ON BECOMING **Nationwide** CONFERENCE CHAMPIONS

Champions!

and in 1997 Cheltenham Town FC was promoted from the Dr Martens League into the GM Vauxhall Conference. The following year the Robins were at Wembley, meeting Southport in the Umbro Trophy Final.

Kick-off for the Sunday spectacular was 3 p.m. and that morning an uninterrupted convoy of coaches, mini buses, vans and cars nose-to-tailed its way along the A40 from Cheltenham to London. The sky was blue, the sun shone and from the window of almost every vehicle red and white scarves fluttered in anticipation. Once inside the home of football, the atmosphere was electric with some 18,000 local fans there to cheer on the heroes they hoped would be victorious. To be truthful, the game was a scrappy affair and for most of it Southport slightly had the upper hand. But then in the seventy-ninth minute, with the score at nil all, there was a goalmouth scramble and Robins' striker Jason Eaton headed the ball into the back of the Southport net. Jubilation! That goal won the game and the trophy. It also overnight turned Cheltenham into a football town.

The Robins missed out on Wembley in 1999, but secured an even greater prize when in May a 6,100 capacity crowd at Whaddon Road cheered the team's promotion to the Football League division three. Celebrations continued with a victory parade on an open-topped bus through the town, where thousands in red and white packed the Prom. Cheltenham's usually genteel premier thoroughfare echoed to the chant of 'Cheltenhamshire – la-la-la!'. It was the greatest day in the Robins' 107-year history – and one of the most memorable for the town.

House Prices

1980
Bournside: neo-Georgian, three-bedroomed town house, lounge/diner, well-equipped kitchen, tidy garden – £21,350
Wyman's Brook: semi-detached with integral garage, three bedrooms, gas central heating – £24,250
Charlton Kings: semi-detached cottage, uninterrupted views to Leckhampton Hill – £25,000
St Mark's: three-bedroomed semi, detached garage – £25,995
Shurdington Road: detached bungalow, three bedrooms, coloured bathroom, detached garage – £34,950

1990
St Lukes: three-bedroomed mid-terrace house with gas central heating – £55,000
Cranham Road: four-bedroomed detached house, gas central heating – £139,000
Prestbury: four-bedroomed detached house in cul-de-sac – £133,950
Fiddlers Green: three-bedroomed modern semi – £63,950
Cleevemount Road: 1930s semi, 100ft garden, garage – £75,000

Datelines

1980   Cheltenham's parks and recreation department reported that Dutch elm disease had wiped out 4,500 trees in the town. The department had just two elms remaining in its care. A new fifty-six bed wing opened at Delancey hospital at a cost of £1 million. On May bank holiday police were called to the Promenade to avert a clash between skinheads and rockers. Whitbread's closed its Cheltenham distribution depot with a loss of forty-seven jobs.

1981   The Everyman celebrated its centenary, but the ABC cinema closed. Summertime street parties celebrated the wedding of Prince Charles to Lady Diana Spencer. And Cheltenham's tourist trade was estimated to be worth £36 million.

1982   Brrr – what a freezer! Cheltenham was colder than Warsaw as the thermometer fell to -4°F (-20.1°C). An armed raider stole £3,000 from the Midland bank at Charlton Kings and made his getaway on a moped. At its first attempt in the Britain in Bloom competition, Cheltenham reached the final and came fourth.

1983   International recession led to local redundancies. Linotype Paul shed 500 jobs and Dowty Mining 400 more. The borough council built a floodlit, all-weather training area on part of the disused railway at Pittville. Demolition work began on the Plough Hotel, one of Cheltenham's oldest buildings, to make way for the Regent Arcade.

1984   The Government banned unions at GCHQ. A long hot summer led to drought conditions and a hose-pipe ban. The Princess of Wales unveiled a plaque to commemorate her visit to the Sue Ryder Home, Leckhampton.

1985   After a £2.5 million refurbishment, the Everyman Theatre re-opened for its Christmas show *Cinderella*. The new GPO sorting office opened in Cheltenham's Swindon Road. The Princess Royal officially opened the Regent Arcade. The Devil's Chimney was shored up at a cost of £25,000. Borough engineer Stan Wadsworth said 'We hope this will make it safe for the next thirty to fifty years.'

1986   Coal merchants Riches & Co. closed its tiny shop in the Prom. Woolworth's closed too amid speculation that a shopping mall was to be built on the High Street site. Unannounced, the South African superstar runner Zola Budd arrived for an athletics meet at the Prince of Wales stadium and smashed the club's 800 metres record by 5.1 seconds.

1987   The Wishing Clock was installed in the main hall of the Regent Arcade. Costing £80,000 and 45ft in height, the world's tallest mechanical clock was designed by Gloucestershire-based artist and writer Kit Williams.

1988   Eagle Star opened its new computer centre at Arle Farm. Plans to develop the Greatfield estate at Up Hatherley on Glebe Farm were approved.

1989   The Cheltenham & Gloucester Building Society sold its Clarence Street headquarters for £7.5 million and moved to Barnwood, Gloucester. A new £1 million stable block for 160 horses was built at Prestbury Park. Charles Irving, MP for Cheltenham since 1974, received a knighthood.

1990   Cheltenham made the record books when the summertime thermometer nudged 98.78°F (37.1°C), the highest temperature ever recorded in Britain.

1991   Cheltenham's population was 101,322. Two security guards were shot and seriously injured outside Lloyds Bank, Bath Road, when their van was the target of a raid. Local horse Garrison Savannah won the Gold Cup. Cheltenham won the Britain in Bloom title.

1992   Signs warning motorists to watch out for toads crossing the A40 appeared at Dowdeswell. The town's ace bowler Tony Allcock became world champion. County-based Pelham Puppets had to double their staff when demand for the firm's Thunderbirds models exceeded supply.

1993	The council tax replaced the poll tax and the average bill in Cheltenham set at £588; however, bills were reduced when the government capped the county council. Woolworth's returned to the High Street. The Cheltenham and County Constitutional Club opened its doors to women for the first time in its ninety-five year history.
1994	Labour Party leader John Smith joined a 10,000 strong march through Cheltenham to mark the tenth anniversary of the ban on unions at GCHQ. Plans were given the go-ahead for a three-storey learning centre at the Park Campus in Cheltenham's conservation area. In an attempt to cheer up Royal Well bus station, the aging concrete shelters were painted with a mural.
1995	Air Chief Marshal Sir Sandy Wilson resigned from the RAF after controversy over the £387,000 redecoration of his official residence near Cheltenham. Master Oats won the Gold Cup. Thousands lined the streets for the civic funeral of Charles Irving, longtime Cheltenham MP.
1996	Three options for the development of the St James's station site went on exhibition in the High Street. Messier-Dowty clinched a multi-million pound deal to make landing gear for the new Bell Boeing 609 hoverplane. The first Cheltenham International Jazz Festival took place.
1997	Linotype-Hell left its Bath Road headquarters. The £10 million Tattersall stand opened at Prestbury Park and Mr Mulligan won the Gold Cup at 20–1. After a thirteen-year ban trade unions were once more permitted at GCHQ.
1998	Brewing came to an end in Cheltenham after a 250-year history, when Whitbreads moved out. Balcarras School was awarded technology college status. Concrete shelters, a feature of Royal Well bus station since 1947, were bulldozed and replaced with modern glass and metal shelters.
1999	GCHQ decided to build its 'millennium doughnut' at Benhall. A record crowd of 146,000 attended the Gold Cup meet. Cheltenham's controversial 'Noddy Train' was axed.

Royal Well bus station was given a makeover in 1998.

EIGHT

In Town Tonight

Cheltenham is a tourist attraction and that's a fact. Forgive the statistics, but annually some six million visitors from all parts of the world come for at least a day, and about 350,000 of them enjoy what they find enough to book themselves in for an overnight stay. While they're here they spend £200 million and by doing so keep 6,000 people working full time in the local tourist trade. That's remarkable. At least it is when you consider that there's no castle, no splendid cathedral and no river to punt on. Cheltenham isn't home to the tallest building in the country, the deepest hole, or any other such record. No William Shakespeare class 'A' list celebrity was born in the town and it hasn't been catapulted to stardom as the setting for a long-running TV series or blockbuster film. So why do people come?

If you're asked where you live and reply 'Cheltenham', the response is almost always 'Oh, that's a nice place'. Sometimes it may be a slightly more enthusiastic: 'What a lovely town. The Promenade is beautiful with all those trees.' Occasionally there'll be a mischievous dig along the lines of 'That's a nice place. Not as nice as Bath, but still nice.' The thing is, the word 'nice' is the one you most often hear. Perhaps this is because the town has never been associated with a particular product or commodity. Sheffield goes with steel. Swindon was a railway town. Coal came from Newcastle. Derby has Rolls-Royce. Towns like to have a motif to go with their name tag in this way. Not so many years ago a sign on the railway station of a Monmouthshire town announced 'Haste ye back to Newport – home of the Mole wrench'. In these post-industrial days many towns and cities that once made Mole wrenches, or whatever, are struggling to establish a new identity. Cheltenham went through the same process more than 150 years ago when the fact that it was the foremost spa in the country was no longer of much interest to anyone. In a way, Cheltenham has been striving to find another identity ever since. That was one reason why some of the dreadful scars that changed the face of the town back in previous decades were allowed to happen. The wounds were self inflicted. For a sleepy 1960s town with low self esteem and no sense of direction the prospect of a huge corporate organisation such as Eagle Star making its headquarters in the town was hugely flattering.

A visitor's guide to Insurance

Standing in landscaped grounds in Bath Road is the imposing Eagle Star House, containing the Group Administrative office and Computer Centre of the Eagle Star Insurance Group. Eagle Star, through its vast network of branch offices throughout the entire country, provides a complete service in all forms of insurance and from this building the administrative decisions affecting the network are put into operation.

Insure with Eagle Star—it pays handsomely!

If we imagine a conversation between Mr Eagle Star and Mr Cheltenham at the time it must have gone something like this:

Mr Eagle Star	'Ah, Cheltenham, step into the board room will you? I'd like to move my administrative headquarters from London to where you are.'
Mr Cheltenham	'Really? Why? – I mean, that's wonderful. When would you like to come?'
Mr Eagle Star	'It will bring a couple of thousand jobs.'
Mr Cheltenham	'Great. When would you like to come?'
Mr Eagle Star	'Add a lot of prestige too. Something to put in your guide book.'
Mr Cheltenham	'Yes, thank you. When would you like to come?'
Mr Eagle Star	'Only thing is we'll have to knock down quite a number of perfectly good Regency buildings that are in harmony with their surroundings and replace them with a concrete and glass multi-storey tower block that will be highly visibly from every aspect and stick out like a wart on supermodel's cheek.'
Mr Cheltenham	'That's fine. You'll be more than welcome.'

The summertime open-air art exhibition in Imperial Gardens is well established in the town's calender.

In years gone by tradespeople were not allowed to enter the Prom. Now regular farmers' markets add an informal bustle that helps to bring tourists to the town.

Lots of other mistakes were made because Cheltenham felt complimented, rather than outraged, when big business promised to make its mark on the town. Yet despite the blemishes, its greatest asset – being perceived as a nice place – remains intact.

There are other perceptions, of course. When Madonna chose Cheltenham Ladies' College for her daughter Lourdes, the American journalist Ambrose Clancy wrote in the Washington Post (19 August 2001) of 'Cheltenham's reputation as being the most conceited town in England', tempering the observation with 'Only the unimaginative or shortsighted would consider this small, beautiful, civilised city [*sic*] stuck-up merely because it embodies the England of Mandarin politeness, Sahara dry humour and discretion.' Then, to make up for any offence caused, he concluded: 'There are opulent

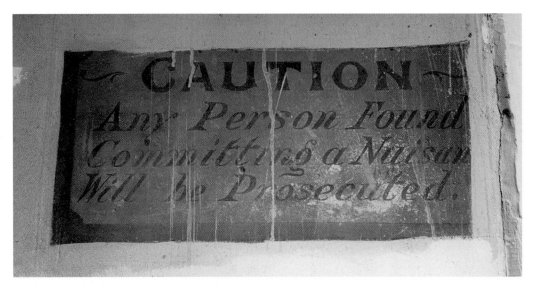

Whingeing has long been a Cheltenham pastime. This Victorian warning is in St Phillips Street.

parks, chic restaurants, boutiques to match London in theatricality and shops where a bell jingles above the door when opened, announcing your entry into the 18th century.'

Although Cheltenham appears to have a stronger sense of its purpose today, it still finds difficulty in pinning down precisely how it wants to present itself. Promotional slogans all in current use include 'The garden town of England', 'Centre for the Cotswolds' and 'The festival town of Britain'. At least Newport knew it was home of the Mole wrench and that was that.

There's no doubt that Cheltenham is very good at inviting visitors, but few would claim the welcome is accompanied by a broad grin and open arms. If you want the Promenade to yourself, go there any afternoon of the March Gold Cup meeting at Prestbury Park. Not wanting to fraternise with racegoers, locals stay away in droves. People who move to the town, especially from parts of the country where some sense of community spirit still thrives, speak of Cheltenham as a deeply unfriendly place. 'I walked into a pub and everyone moved away from the bar', a friend who came here from Lancashire with his job seventeen years ago told me.

Something else incomers find extraordinary is the Cheltenham–Gloucester divide. They're bemused that two centres of population, both about the same size and 7 miles apart, barely acknowledge one another's presence. Finding mention of our neighbouring city in the local press is a fairly recent novelty and just about the only official contact between the two councils is when they meet to disagree about the future of Gloucestershire Airport, which they own jointly. The difference between Cheltenham and Gloucester is illustrated by the licence fee each charges to snack van traders. To set up your motorised hot dog stall in Gloucester will set you back £531. In Cheltenham the fee is £5,781, and you're not allowed to blight the town centre with your burgers, only the outlying parts.

If you talk to people who deal with the public in Cheltenham it's not usually long before the word 'whingers' crops up. There's evidence to back up the accusation too. The local government ombudsman receives significantly more complaints from people in Cheltenham than any other town in the south west, or for virtually any similar sized town in the country. Cheltenham is free ranging and catholic in its whingeing, as a glimpse of the letters page in the local newspaper reveals. Let's take a peek at subjects that have been raised recently (summer 2002). There we find a person who contacted the council some while ago because the lamp posts in her street needed painting, then wrote again to complain that now they had been and she didn't like the colour. Children eating crisps on buses aroused the ire of one correspondent, which sparked a series of letters on the same subject, including one that observed 'I have never come across so many drivers with so little control of what goes on in their buses'. A former domestic science teacher berated the newspaper for inaccuracy over the ingredients of spotted dick. 'I would like to correct one point in your article. Spotted dick traditionally is not a sponge mix. It is made with a slack suet dough.' Plans to clad the Art Gallery and Museum in steel sheet had many people stretching for their quills, among them the writer of 'I am sure that I cannot be the only resident in Cheltenham who is strongly opposed to having the equivalent of an expensive biscuit tin in Clarence Street. Why is it that we now seem to cater for the flashiest and the cheapest type of street architecture?' One possible reason why local folk do so much whingeing is that they've got the time. From a population of a little over 100,000, nearly 30 per cent of all households in the town are made up of retired people living on their own.

Something else that new arrivals to the town find curious is the way people speak. Many towns in the country have an indigenous accent, but Cheltenham has two. One is the featureless, standard southern received pronunciation heard pretty well anywhere in Britain now, while the other is an urbanised version of the Gloucestershire accent. These two voices are heard separately, but rarely in conversation with one another. They hardly ever come into contact, because they live in different places. To define where each group resides, draw a line running roughly north east/south west from Prestbury, through Boots Corner to the Reddings (with a bit of a dog's leg to take in parts of Pittville). The received pronunciation speakers live south of this line, the urban Gloucestershire speakers live north of it.

Cheltenham has been two towns since its heyday as a spa and remains so. The contrast is profound. House prices in the leafy parts are among the highest in the country, but one ward in the town ranks among the UK's top twenty most deprived areas. As a regional retail destination, Cheltenham is a premier league player, yet more than half of the 16,000 people who live in its 5,500 council houses are on benefits.

In the mid-1990s the borough council put together a detailed study of the Lower High Street prior to its bid for funding of the regeneration scheme. This revealed that most of the houses, which were built in the nineteenth century, were owner-occupied by residents who were either retired or unemployed. A quarter of the people here claimed housing, or council tax benefit and a fifth of them were struggling on an annual income of under £3,000. The study also highlighted that 25 per cent of the population in this quarter of town had problems reading and writing. For a town with an economy that is buoyant and thriving, such findings represent quite a skeleton in the cupboard. Since 1996, when the Lower High Street, or High Street West End as it's now known in official circles (and nowhere else), was designated a neighbourhood renewal area by the borough council, a programme to improve housing and environmental conditions has been underway. It must be said that visible improvements have been made. Shops and houses have been brightened up, redundant buildings such as the Wesleyan chapel in St George's Street and the former Devonshire Street school have been converted into flats, while CCTV and neighbourhood watch schemes have been put in place. Small businesses are being encouraged to move to this part of town as well.

Similar schemes are afoot in other parts of the town that tourists never see. The high-rise flats along Shakespeare Road that were some of the first built in Hesters Way and well past their sell-by date have been pulled down and replaced by housing on a

Gloucestershire College of Art and Technology moved to Princess Elizabeth Way. The site was previously occupied by Monkscroft School.

Sochi Court, Hesters Way. Regeneration partnerships in Whaddon, Lynworth, Lower High Street and Hesters Way are underway and much needed.

much more human scale. The development of the former Monkscroft Secondary School site has introduced better quality housing and the move by Gloucestershire College of Art and Technology (Gloscat) from The Park to a new, purpose-built campus at Hesters Way brings vibrancy, function and prestige to the area. Perhaps the increased presence of GCHQ will help to raise the profile as well.

To its credit, the town council appears to be making a genuine effort to fund investment in parts of Cheltenham that badly need it. Regeneration partnerships have been set up in Whaddon, Lynworth, Hesters Way and the Lower High Street, while practical efforts are in hand to try to control crime. What will happen when the funding stops and these areas are left to fend for themselves once more remains to be seen. But it could be that the neighbourhood colleges now in operation in Cheltenham's less leafy parts that are providing adult training and education hold the key. Back in the nineteenth century Dean Close knew that education was the route out of poverty, and the same holds true today for sections of the community who feel disenfranchised.

*   *   *

Cheltenham has one of the strongest economies in the south west and at the time of writing unemployment is less than 2 per cent. For a town with no history as an industrial

The GCHQ 'Doughnut', Benhall.

centre, it's surprising that there are more blue-collar workers in the town than in Gloucester. Around a fifth of the town's 62,000-strong workforce (more than half are women by the way) are employed in manufacturing, which is a higher percentage than the national average. They work for companies that specialise in high precision metal engineering that produce sub-contracted components for the aerospace industry. Economists would say this is a vulnerable position to be in, because when big names in the sector such as Smiths Industries and Dowty are hit by worldwide recession, their specialist suppliers are affected adversely by the knock on. This happened in the early 1990s when the Berlin wall came down ending the cold war. Other places received a share of the peace dividend, but in Cheltenham redundancies were the result.

GCHQ is the biggest single employer, providing some 4,000 jobs, but the financial and business services sector – banking, insurance, law, accountancy, estate agents, computer services – keeps the highest percentage (28 per cent) of people in work. For those who enjoy statistics 21 per cent of jobs in Cheltenham are in public services, 18 per cent in distribution, hotels and catering, 4 per cent in construction and 2 per cent in communications and transport. If Stagecoach had its way that final figure would, no doubt, be a good deal higher, as it constantly struggles to find enough drivers for its buses.

In the referendum of June 2001 the town voted no to the idea of a directly elected mayor. Since then the borough has been run by a leader who appoints a team of between five and seven executives to decide policy, which then has to be wrangled over by the full council. The annual budget of around £12 million is raised by council tax, business rates and government grants, and one or two perks. Car parking – among the most expensive outside London – turns in a profit of nearly £2 million a year, for example.

A pressing problem is how to preserve the character of Cheltenham while allowing for change. New service companies are desirable to broaden the economic base of the town and make it less dependent on manufacturing or any other single sector, but at the same time the town's heritage must be protected if Cheltenham is to remain a sought after place to be and a destination for tourists. Growth is inevitable as the town is required by government to build some 7,000 new houses by 2011. Tewkesbury Borough Council's boundary extends to the edge of Cheltenham, and it's likely that significant numbers of new houses will appear on the Badgeworth, Leckhampton and Shurdington side of town. Cheltenham is bounded by green belt and the designated Cotswold Area of Outstanding Natural Beauty, so space for residential or employment development is hard to find. Inevitably this places an emphasis on developing land

Cheltenham's economy is more dependent on manufacturing than the national average. It's the town's policy to attract employers in other sectors, such as the computer services company Marlborough Sterling (shown here), which is based at the St James's station site.

within the town, rather than at its outskirts, and as few people (except builders) want to see our open spaces gobbled up by brick and tarmac it may be the preferable option. It does, however, create a special difficulty in a place such as Cheltenham.

Outside the 600-hectare Central Conservation Area, which covers most of the town centre, Pittville and Lansdown, there are many large houses that stand in good-sized plots. Actually, there aren't nearly so many as there used to be because a good number of them now have houses standing in what used to be the garden. The usual pattern is that a building company approaches the owner of such a property (or the other way round) and a deal is struck to make an application for planning permission. Typically, two planning applications are put in, starting with one to demolish the existing house altogether and build on the whole plot. The first neighbours know about this is when they see the planning application notice go up on the fence outside. It invites people to inspect the proposed plans at the Municipal Offices and write a letter outlining their objections if they have any. Locals are then galvanised into action and send off their letters, or even organise a petition. In the meantime the owner and building company make a second planning application – to keep the existing house, which may be a landmark building in the area, and build in its garden instead. By now the business has been going on for a goodly time and the objectors are wearied. They comfort themselves with a partial victory ('Well, we stopped them pulling the whole thing down, didn't we?') and the second application is passed by the planning committee. The owner of the house now sells it and moves, if possible to a similar property with a large garden so that the exercise can be repeated. The building company puts up its houses in the garden and sells them. Both parties make a heap of cash – and the character of the town has been changed irreparably. This kind of infill increases the density of housing, puts more cars into a locality and often spoils the architectural unity of a neighbourhood. Greed fuels the process and that's never a pleasant motive, but it's difficult to blame owners of such properties from selling off their gardens for development. After all, there's no law against it. But what a good idea it would be to introduce one.

There are six conservation areas in Cheltenham and the most recent of them received its designation in May 2001. When the part council, part private St Marks housing estate was built during the 1920s all the roads were named after poets. There was no particular reason for this and the choice was a touch arbitrary. Alfred Lord Tennyson and Cecil Day-Lewis both lived in Cheltenham and both were poet laureates, but while the former had a road named in his honour, the latter didn't. For whatever reason, the Poets' Conservation Area (perhaps to call it the St Mark's Conservation Area didn't sound grand enough) came into being and deservedly so. The estate is a good example of between-the-wars housing, and present-day developers could learn a lesson or two from the way homes of different styles complement each other. Some are terraced, others semi-detached, and the influence of the Arts and Crafts movement can be glimpsed in their gables, rooflines and design details. Designation gave a voice to the

Byron Road, St Marks.

view that it's not only the great estates of Lansdown, Bayshill, Montpellier and Pittville that have a place in the town's heritage.

There was irony in the timing of the borough council's five-year town plan, which was titled 'Our town, our future – Cheltenham 2000 to 2005' and included the declaration that 'We expect new buildings to be well designed and to improve the appearance of our town'. At the time of publication Century Court in Bath Road had just been finished, all bar the making good, and had refired the modern versus replica architecture debate that rumbles round Cheltenham on almost every occasion that a large and visible new building appears. There was no denying that the luxury flats were entirely out of keeping with their surroundings in design and materials, and the debate was particularly strenuous for a number of reasons. Those against the development pointed out that this kind of mistake had been allowed to happen within a stone's throw of the Eagle Star tower block, thus proving that unlike lightning, planners' madness could strike in the same place twice. Then there was the fact that this uncompromisingly contemporary range of apartments on one side of the road squared up to the uncompromisingly gothic range of Cheltenham College on the other like a mocking reflection.

Century Court, Bath Road, refired the modern versus replica debate on architecture.

On a much smaller scale the same confrontation of architectural styles took place a year or two later in Vittoria Walk, when a square-lined, blunt-faced modern courtyard development was built directly opposite the bow-fronted, elegantly detailed Regency house that is the town's oldest spa building.

Neither Century Court nor the Vittoria Walk development caused as much venting of spleen in Cheltenham as the Millennium Restaurant. To the astonishment of many, permission was granted for this construction in Portland Street in the late 1990s. Now some fearsome boobs have been made by the town's planners in the past half century, but the Millennium Restaurant sent the needle of the boobometer whizzing off the scale. Developed by a local builder and designed, so it appeared, by a child suffering from too many sci-fi cartoons, the building was plainly intended as a nightclub. Although permission had been granted for the thing to be built, the council got shirty about it being a club. The restaurant closed after nine months with debts of £200,000 and was then boarded up. Every so often a consortium comes along and declares it wants to turn the place into a health club, bingo hall, or something else. Some misguided soul even wanted it as a private house. But really everyone knows that the best purpose to which the Millennium Restaurant can be put is as hardcore for a new road somewhere.

The new . . .

. . . confronts the old in Vittoria Walk.

The Millennium restaurant, one of Cheltenham's worst architectural mistakes.

Millennium Restaurant and one or two other aberrations apart, since the Royscot House episode of the late 1980s when the town insisted on a building that would blend, rather than contrast with its period surroundings, replica Regency has been the preferred option in Cheltenham. Even so, developments such as Century Court in Bath Road appear, and are reminders that a close eye needs to be kept on officials who supposedly have the best interests of the town at heart.

Apart from the GCHQ doughnut, the biggest development in twenty-first-century Cheltenham was on the site of St James's station, which had remained vacant since the mid-1960s when the railway was removed. Stretching from St James's Square in the town centre through to Gloucester Road, this large tract of land brought the Waitrose Food and Home store to town. The retailer originally had its eye on land near the Golden Valley bypass previously owned by Dowty, but eventually it agreed to come into town rather than join other superstores on the boundary. Perhaps the most interesting aspect of the St James's site development was the new housing built at the Gloucester Road end to spur the regeneration of the west end of town.

Just as debate about how St James's should be developed rumbled on for decades, the former Black and White coach station site in St Margaret's Road remains the object of ongoing speculation. Suggestions are made and discarded regularly, but one that perhaps deserved a second thought was the idea of building new Municipal Offices there. The present prominent Promenade position has been occupied by the council for almost a century and the building must be less efficient for its function than a purpose-built block would be. This would also leave the prestigiously placed Prom offices vacant for another purpose, a town centre hotel for example, which would add life to the town centre round the clock instead of standing empty from 6 p.m. until 9 a.m., and make a contribution to the town's coffers.

*   *   *

Traffic and the pollution it causes have always been problems in Cheltenham. Back in the days of horse-drawn buses there were vociferous complaints about the dung and the clatter of hooves. When electric trams arrived objections were raised about the unsightly overhead wires, and when trams were superseded by motor buses people became exercised about the fumes and the dangers. The unavoidable problem today is that we have twenty-first-century traffic on a nineteenth-century road system. That's

The acceptable face of Regency replica in Montpellier Spa Road.

What were the town planners thinking of? This pretty town villa in Park Place by the eminent nineteenth-century architect J.B. Papworth is nudged in the back by the Nat West Bank offices, designed by someone who had a job lot of unwanted concrete slabs going cheap.

the cause of the problem, but schemes are constantly introduced that tinker with the symptoms, such as speed bumps, traffic 'calming' measures, intricate patterns painted on the roads and big signs screwed to lamp-posts telling drivers that they should walk or ride a bike. These tinkerings go in and out of fashion, and the most recent favourite is the mini roundabout. Only a short time ago Cheltenham was a stranger to the mini roundabout, but now they're everywhere – and almost without exception serve to create even longer traffic jams than there were before.

During the morning and evening rush hours there are some **33,000** people sitting in cars on local roads: **20,000** of them are commuting into and the rest commuting out of Cheltenham. Desirable though it might be to reduce the number of cars moving in and out of the town centre, this simply won't happen unless the public transport system improves almost beyond imagining. It's a telling fact that 75 per cent of people in town live within 3 miles of where they work, but the majority of them travel by car. They know this will inevitably involve sitting in tailbacks, use petrol inefficiently and cost a fortune in car park charges. They know it's environmentally unfriendly, bad for the blood pressure and could even put them on the wrong end of an act of road rage. But they also know that there's no real option, because the public transport system in Cheltenham is far from wonderful. It's difficult to find anyone with a good word to say for the buses. The bus operators constantly claim their inability to deliver a reasonable service is caused by a lack of drivers.

And then there's the simple fact that the buses don't go where people want them to go. A long-running saga reported in the local newspapers concerned a gent who lived at Leckhampton and had the modest desire to do his shopping in Safeway at Greatfield Park. The distance from his home to the supermarket as the crow flies was no more than 1 mile. To reach his destination by bus presented him with two options, neither of them attractive. He either caught the Brockworth bus, which would take him half way, and walk the rest (passing a newly installed mini roundabout, of course). Or he caught a bus into the town centre, trekked across to the stop for the Warden Hill service and waited for it to arrive, then carried on to the supermarket. As the gent was of riper years, the prospect of struggling half a mile loaded up with the week's provisions ruled out the first option. The second was expensive, because it involved paying for two return journeys, and time consuming, because of the circuitous route and four spells of waiting in a bus queue for the round trip. To add spice to the business, there was the very real possibility that one of his connections would be axed while our hero was pushing his trolley round the aisles making it impossible for him to bring home the bacon. Faced with such tribulation, many of us would shrug our shoulders, succumb to defeat and accept that

Waitrose development nearing completion on the St James's station site, summer 2002.

the joy of Safeway was no longer open to us. But our man from Leckhampton was made of sterner stuff and took his case to the local parish council, the county council, championed the cause by letter, created his own formidable PR machine, and made personal representations. After four years of this his effort bore fruit when a bus company agreed to operate a once weekly service from Leckhampton to Safeway. The bus company that agreed came from Stroud, by the way. The Cheltenham-based Stagecoach operator couldn't do it. They probably didn't have enough drivers.

*   *   *

Churchgoing remains a more prominent feature of Cheltenham life than in most towns and the evangelical tradition seems to have strengthened in recent times, perhaps because of religious initiatives such as the Alpha Project. It's a tradition that can be traced back to the nineteenth century when an organisation called the Simeon Trust bought the rights to appoint ministers from landed gentry who previously owned the privilege. This Trust appoints the ministers, favouring those of an evangelical persuasion, for about a dozen churches in and around Cheltenham town centre. On the outskirts of town more people B & Q of a Sunday than C of E, but in the evangelical stronghold the congregations are flourishing. There are some sixty places of worship in the town spanning pretty well the full gambit of religions – C of E, Baptist, Christadelphian, Christian Brethren, Christian Science, Congregational, Jewish, Methodist, Muslim, Roman Catholic, Salvation Army, Society of Friends, Unitarian, United Reformed, Latter Day Saints, Elim Pentecostal, Jehovah's Witnesses, Spiritualists, the New Apostolic Church and a few more besides. Plenty of choice in other words.

*   *   *

Cheltenham can justifiably claim to be one the UK's leading festival towns. The calendar of events is year round, starting with the New Year's Day race meeting, a folk festival in February and the National Hunt Festival ('Gold Cup Week') in March is attended by 100,000 race goers. The International Jazz Festival is now established in April, followed by the Competitive Arts Festival and Science Week. The Festival of Music, accompanied by its fringe, takes place in July, as does the Cricket Festival. Sequence dancers bounce around the Town Hall in August and have just about enough time to pack away their sparkly costumes before the ballroom dancers arrive for their gathering in September. In October famous authors descend to sell as many of their books as possible at the Festival of Literature, Murphy's sponsors the November race

Opposite: Montpellier. Cappuccinoland by day, lagerland by night.

St James's church, Suffolk Square, could be given a new lease of life – as a nightclub?

meet and December is illuminated by the festival of Christmas lights.

This eclectic flurry of festivals collectively brings hundreds of thousands of people to the town, but in addition to these there's another festival that takes place every Friday and Saturday night of the year: the Cheltenham Festival of Stella Artois. Now firmly established as the Ibiza of the south west, the town plays host to some 20,000 pubbers and clubbers who come from as far away as Bristol, Birmingham and Oxford to avail themselves of the pleasures on tap in eighty-seven licensed premises, plus fifteen nightclubs within the inner ring road alone. Pop along for the music and you have the choice of such splendidly named genres as hip hop, break beat, drum 'n' bass, funky house, trance and UK garage (excuse me if I'm telling you things you already know). Montpellier is at the hub of things. During the day this continental quarter of town is as decorous as its caryatids, a place to sip cappuccino and check the share prices. But come eight o'clock on a weekend evening things liven up no end. The generation that grew up with Mrs Thatcher's pronouncement that there is no such thing as society ringing in their ears plainly took her at her word. If there's no such thing as society, then society won't mind if you pee on its doorstep. A report by the Cheltenham and Gloucester College of Higher Education, now proudly reborn as the University of Gloucestershire, came to the conclusion that all this jollity puts £30 million over local bars. The bars pay business taxes, so the town's economy benefits and that's not to be sniffed at. Neither are town centre telephone boxes after closing time if you're of a sensitive disposition. When there's money on this scale to be made, it's hardly surprising that plans for new bars and clubs are put forward all the time. So many, in fact, that the borough council had to announce plans to restrict the number of clubs and clamp down on cheap drink promotions designed to pull people in.

Many would say that crowds of people milling about the Regency parts engaging in hedonistic pursuits is not at all Cheltenham. But actually it is. The town centre has long been a leisure resort, a place to seek pleasure, to see and be seen. In spa days they came to take the waters. Now they come to take the lagers.

Index

(Bold figures give page numbers of pictures)